10-SECOND SUPERPOWER

How the Game-Changing Secret of Magic
Questions® Can Transform Your Work,
Wealth, Relationships, and Your Entire Life

KEITH ELLIS

Special Offer for Readers of This Book

People learn the game-changing secrets of the *10-Second Superpower*® in different ways. Some like to read. Others prefer an audiobook. And some would rather work directly with the #1 Superpower Coach™ in the world and bestselling author Keith Ellis, within a community of good-hearted people who are creating and sharing the most powerful *Magic Questions* in the world.

If you'd like to join Keith in this groundbreaking online experience, visit here to claim this once-in-a-lifetime offer:

SPECIAL OFFER:

The Magic Questions® Goldmine

https://www.magicquestionsgoldmine.com/special-offer-for-readers-of-10ssp

If you have more time to listen than to read, you can take advantage of a limited-time-only offer for the audiobook version of

10-SECOND SUPERPOWER, narrated by the author, Keith Ellis, the #1 Superpower Coach™ in the world:

SPECIAL OFFER for the audiobook

https://www.10secondsuperpower.com/special-offer-for-audiobook

If you'd like another copy of this book, or to give one as a gift, you can find it on Amazon here:

10-SECOND SUPERPOWER

https://a.co/d/8zdvxov

Copyright

Distribution

The paperback version of this book is available from Ingram for distribution to bookstores, wholesalers, libraries, and educational institutions.

https://www.ingramcontent.com/

Disclaimer

Magic Questions® are powerful stuff.

The Author and the Publisher assume absolutely NO liability of any kind whatsoever for any thoughts or actions that may result or be said to result from anything written or referenced herein.

Additionally, the Author and the Publisher make absolutely NO warranty or claims of any kind whatsoever, stated or implied, for anything written or referenced herein.

More importantly, if you're worried about a disclaimer, then please DO NOT READ THIS BOOK, because you're not ready for it.

Magic Questions® and the *10-Second Superpower™* are designed to help you take charge of your life, not blame someone else if you don't.

BE WARNED:

If you do choose to continue reading this book, you proceed entirely at your own risk.

If you choose not to read it, the same applies.

Dedication

To Rick, Al, and Stu, the best brothers anyone could have, and the best friends I could ever imagine

Acknowledgements

Special thanks to Alan Ellis, Rick Ellis, Helen English Guthrie, and Dr. Robert K. Guthrie for their invaluable comments and suggestions at various phases of this project.

Table of Contents

Book 7: THE MAGIC OF PEOPLE

Prologue

*H*ave you ever wondered why your life isn't turning out the way you thought it would?

Well guess what?

IT'S NOT YOUR FAULT

I know, I know, this flies in the face of all the conventional wisdom we've been taught about success. But have you ever asked yourself, why is it that conventional wisdom doesn't seem to work for most people?

I have. I've spent most of my adult life asking this question. And I finally discovered the answer.

Let me explain.

Some years ago, I found myself in what could generously be described as a midlife crisis.

My friends and family seemed to think I was successful, which was nice and all, but at best I was nothing more than "success adjacent". Always a bridesmaid, so to speak, but never quite a bride.

I was a success junkie, and I studied everything I could find about self improvement, self-help, and personal empowerment. I even practiced what the experts preached. But no matter how hard I worked, I was always coming up just shy of the big career break-through that I'd always dreamed about.

Do you know what I mean?

The good news is that I was blessed with an amazing wife and family, a solid job, and a lovely home in the beautiful foothills of the Blue Ridge Mountains.

What more could a person ask for, right?

But that was the problem. Even with all that going for me, I still felt like something was missing. My life just wasn't working out the way I had planned.

What I had was good, but deep in my heart I wanted great. No, not just great, I wanted *extraordinary*. And I knew it was out there, just waiting for me. I could almost taste it. But no matter what I did or whose advice I followed it just didn't happen for me.

Then one icy morning at the beginning of January I was paging through the weekly business section in the newspaper and stumbled across an article about a start-up company that was developing some intriguing new software. I was in the software business myself, and halfway through the article I realized that this new technology was going to change the world.

I'd always dreamed of being part of something like that, so it was no surprise that my heart began to beat a little faster. I remember thinking, "Wow, I wish I could join them! Since I'm already in their industry, maybe I could convince them to hire me!"

As intoxicating as this thought was, the next one that came along crushed the life out of it:

There's absolutely no way I can do that.

I knew that I couldn't uproot us from our little slice of paradise and move us back to the big city. No way on earth.

Sigh.

Then a simple question sprang to mind:

But what if I could?

This stopped me dead in my tracks. What an absolutely prepos-terous notion! Even to consider the possibility was absurd.

And yet, before I knew what was happening, instead of feeling sorry for myself I was happily trying to figure out how I could join the little company I'd just read about.

As a plan began to form in my mind, I knew that the first thing I had to do was ask my wife what she thought about my sudden onset of insanity. When I finally tracked her down (it was a big house) I told her what was on my mind, crossed my fingers, and waited.

Margie responded with one of her breathtaking smiles. By a bizarre coincidence, she was having a similar morning to mine. An old friend had just called her from the job she'd left behind when we'd moved to the country many years before, and asked if there were any way she would consider coming back to work in the big city. By the time I told her what I was thinking about, Margie was already way ahead of me. (Not the first time, by the way, and certainly not the last.)

As fast as I could type I updated my resume and emailed it to the CEO of that little start-up company. They hired me, and Margie's friend hired her.

A few short weeks later we had moved out of our spacious home in paradise, put most of what we owned in storage, and crammed ourselves into a tiny, one-bedroom apartment in the city, where we promptly began our new jobs.

The start-up I joined was named webMethods. I was their sixth employee.

This was back when the World Wide Web was just beginning to reinvent the world, and anything seemed possible. But it didn't take long for me to begin to wonder if I had bitten off more than I could chew. As the newly minted vice-president of sales my job was to sell a product that wasn't finished, from a company no one had ever heard of, to a market that didn't exist.

I struggled.

Not surprisingly, within a few months our little company was running low on money. As a professional salesperson I was in the business of asking other people questions, so I decided to ask myself one:

How can I help us generate more revenue?

OMG! It felt like I'd flipped a switch in my brain.

For months all I'd been doing night and day was trying to generate more revenue for our struggling company. But I'd never actually asked myself this simple little question, at least not in so many words.

The moment I did, it was like fireworks in my brain. Answers began occurring to me, one after another, until I suddenly encountered an idea that would become an absolute game changer. We needed a Hail Mary, and I knew that this was it:

We have to become famous

If everybody knew our name, then it would become so much easier for us to get in the door to sell what we had to offer. And not incidentally, it would also make it easier to raise money. Two big wins for the price of one!

I felt like I was on a roll with this question thing, so I asked myself another one:

How can I make us famous overnight?

This wasn't part of my job description, of course, but the question didn't seem to care because the answer appeared as if by magic. I realized that the easiest way to become famous is to join forces with somebody who's already famous. Someone who can lend their reputation to yours. If we could get a person like that to endorse what we were doing, then our company's odds of success would skyrocket.

So I asked myself:

Who can help us become famous?

Again, like magic I somehow knew the answer. There was only one person in our embryonic industry who was already a rock star. His name was Tim Berners-Lee. He had literally invented the World Wide Web. If I could somehow get him to endorse us then we would be in a fantastic position.

But there was one small problem. I didn't know him and I didn't know anybody who did. I would have googled him, but Google wasn't around yet. I would have tried to connect with him on Facebook or LinkedIn, but they didn't exist.

I was clueless, not to mention desperate, so I asked myself yet another question:

How can I get in front of Tim Berners-Lee?

Wow, more magic!

No sooner had I asked this question than I came across an ad for a trade conference in New York City that was only a couple weeks away. By an incredible coincidence, my guy was scheduled to be the keynote speaker! If I could attend that conference, then maybe I could figure out a way to meet him and convince him to help us.

Grasping at that straw, when the date arrived two of us headed to Manhattan.

We reached the show floor just in time to set up our display. I left my colleague to handle the booth and hustled to the keynote presentation that was about to begin. My foolproof plan was to persuade the most famous man in our industry to come back to our little booth and see what we had. I just hadn't figured out how to do that yet.

The auditorium was humming with the anticipation of a crowd waiting for a celebrity to appear. But the moment Tim Berners-Lee walked onstage and began to speak I could tell something was wrong. He must have had a terrible cold or the flu, or maybe both because he sounded awful. He kept pausing to hack and sneeze, but he soldiered on.

When he finished, like any rock star he was mobbed by his fans, clamoring to meet the man whose technology was even then transforming the human experience. I stood on the periphery, watching, while his other admirers had their way with him. Every interaction seemed to drain a portion of what little energy he had left, but he never refused to shake a hand or respond to a question.

My turn finally came when everyone else had gone. I could tell that Tim was exhausted. Yet to my everlasting shame all I could think about was how to drag this weary soul back to our booth so I could show him the technology we were developing.

And I still didn't know how I could entice him to do that.

Just shy of too late, a question flashed into my brain:

What can I offer such an important person?

My mind began to race. I was already shaking his hand when the most magical answer of all materialized. Naturally, it was another question:

What if I offered him a piece of our company?

Bingo! That was it!

Of course, I had no authority to make such an offer, not without consulting our stockholders. But then again, what were the odds that a man of his stature would even listen to me? He invented the Web for heaven's sake! As long as I was totally up front with him about it I had nothing to lose. And if for some crazy reason he said *yes*, well, maybe I could convince our stockholders to go along. As the saying goes, it's easier to get forgiveness than permission.

Tim was obviously on his last legs, but he greeted me graciously, even kindly. I have no idea how he summoned the energy to do that, but I took a deep breath and launched into my 30-second elevator pitch about what our amazing engineers were creating.

His face lit up. "You're building a semantic network!" he said. "That's just what the Web needs!"

I was stunned by such a positive reaction, so I plunged ahead and asked if he would be interested in joining our board of advisors in return for some stock options, provided I could somehow persuade our stockholders to approve.

Tim smiled. "I'd be very interested," he said as we turned and headed toward my company's booth. "I may have helped create the Web, but I've never made a penny from it."

Life has changed profoundly since then, thanks in large part to what Tim invented. Five billion people now use the World Wide Web in one form or another. Religion doesn't spread that fast. Tim is no longer just a rock star, he's a legend. He's not even Tim anymore. He is Sir Timothy John Berners-Lee, knighted by Queen Elizabeth of Great Britain because of how profoundly he changed the world. In a recent ranking of the cultural moments that have done the most to shape human history, a panel of eminent thinkers rated the invention of the World Wide Web as the most important of them all.[1]

Three years after the trade conference webMethods went public in one of the largest software IPOs in history. Sir Timothy finally received some long-overdue compensation for the amazing gift he had bestowed upon the world.

And I learned something I will never forget. This is the secret I'm about to share with you.

Book 1: THE 10-SECOND SUPERPOWER

1

How can I change my life at the speed of thought?

*I*n his classic audio program *"The Strangest Secret"* Earl Nightingale explained that the key to getting what we want from life is to understand this most basic principle of human nature:

You become what you think about

Whoever you are, whatever you feel, whatever you do, it's all based on what you think about.

It's sort of like driving a car. A car goes where you steer it. If you steer it in a different direction, it goes in a different direction, all 4,000 pounds of it. It can't go anywhere else.

Our brain works in exactly the same fashion. Our thoughts are the steering wheel. If we want our life to go in a different direction, then first we have to turn our thoughts in a different direction.

This simple principle is the foundation of everything we are, everything we feel, and everything we do. And yet not one in a thousand of us even know it exists.

That is strange. What makes it even stranger is that this "secret" has been around for a long time. Nightingale credited his insight to a book published in 1903, <u>As a Man Thinketh</u>, by James Allen, whose inspiration, in turn, went all the way back to a passage in the Bible.[1] So this life-changing insight into human nature has been around for thousands of years, and yet it's still a secret.

Don't believe that? Then consider the people around you. Do any of them ever complain? Have you ever heard anyone say something like this:

"I'm tired!"

"I'm depressed!"

"I'm frustrated!"

"I'm angry!"

"I'm so unhappy!"

Perhaps you've even said these things yourself from time to time. You are human, after all, and we humans do an awful lot of this.

What's crazy is that when we think thoughts like these we are literally programming our brain to feel tired, depressed, frustrated, unhappy, and angry. If we do it long enough then we actually become these things—tired, depressed, frustrated, unhappy, and angry—which is precisely the opposite of what we really want. Now *that's* the strangest secret.

Fortunately, the same secret that made you who you are can make you who you want to be.

Magic Questions Are Your 10-Second Superpower

In the *Prologue*, I shared how I met Sir Timothy Berners-Lee, the inventor of the World Wide Web, and what this remarkable experience taught me about asking questions. After that happened I became obsessed with questions. I wanted to understand what gives them so much power in our minds and our lives.

Over time, I identified certain types of questions that were especially potent. I analyzed and tested dozens of these on myself, and produced such amazing outcomes in my life that I began to think of them as *Magic Questions*. It felt like they gave me a superpower I never knew I had.

Even better, I developed a drop-dead simple strategy for how to ask myself *precisely* the right question, in *precisely* the right way, at *precisely* the right time. The result was a game-changer.

When I shared this secret with others, they began to produce such amazing outcomes in their own lives that I found myself wondering, if *Magic Questions* are so powerful, and yet so incredibly easy to use, how could I be the only person in history to have figured this out?

But of course, I wasn't.

As I mentioned earlier, I've always been a success junkie. My mission in life is to unlock my own potential, and to help others unlock theirs.

When I began to study *Magic Questions*, I revisited the reams of success literature I'd accumulated through the years to see if questions like these had popped up anywhere else.

Turns out they appeared almost *everywhere* else. *Magic Questions* are at the heart of every personal development philosophy I've ever encountered, from Socrates to Tony Robbins. One way or another, all of the wisdom of success is based on *Magic Questions*.

If conventional wisdom isn't working for you, it's not your fault, *it's your questions*. Because you haven't yet learned the missing ingredient for success: *Magic Questions*.

Trying to succeed without using *Magic Questions* is like trying to spell the word "success" without vowels, it just won't work.

So let's call a spade a spade. The key to making every other success system work is *Magic Questions®*.

Nobody else calls them that, of course, and nobody else seems to realize that this particular type of question, asked in this specific way, is the key to making their own success systems work.

But it doesn't really matter what the "experts" call them, because *Magic Questions* are behind everything they teach.

Magic Questions, by any other name, are still *Magic Questions*. If you learn how to ask yourself precisely the right question, in precisely the right way, at precisely the right time, then you'll unlock the key to getting everything you want from life. I know this sounds like an exaggeration, but it's not. If anything, it's an understatement.

To make a long story a little bit shorter, after years of research and experimentation, I finally isolated why *Magic Questions* are indispensable to every other framework for success.

What *Magic Questions* do better than any other tool on earth is empower us to change what we think about.

Why is this such a big deal?

Because when we're stuck in a bad place emotionally or psychologically, it can be incredibly hard to change what we're thinking about. When we're thinking the wrong thoughts, it feels almost impossible to think the right ones. And when we are thinking the wrong thoughts, it is absolutely impossible to get the right results.

Perhaps you have some first-hand knowledge of this. Have you ever felt stuck?

I have. Far more times than I care to admit.

If you ever find yourself feeling overwhelmed, or afraid, or angry, or helpless, or any other self-defeating thoughts that grab hold of you and won't let go, then *Magic Questions* are the tools you need to pry your thoughts and your feelings away from being stuck, so you can move forward in the direction you want your life to go, instead of being stranded where you are.

In other words, the easiest way to change your life is to change your thoughts, and the easiest way to change your thoughts is to ask yourself *Magic Questions*.

That's because questions are the most powerful catalyst there is for changing what we think about. Whatever is on our mind, when we're asked a question it's hard not to think about answering it.

Like this one:

Why is it important for you to be reading this right now?

Questions are such a critical component of our thinking that it's not unreasonable to suggest that questions are quite literally *how* we think. What makes *Magic Questions* so special is that they empower us to think about what we want to think about, instead of what we don't.

It all comes down to this:

You are what you think about

If you want to change anything in your life, first you have to change your thoughts. If you want to change your thoughts, change your questions.

Life really is as simple as that.

That doesn't mean it's easy. You can't change everything in your life all at once just by changing your thoughts, any more than you can fly from New York to Hawaii just by thinking about it.

In fact, thinking about change is never enough. You have to turn your new thoughts into actions. You can't change your life solely from thinking differently, you have to act differently. But you won't act differently *until* you think differently. That's what the vast majority of human beings fail to understand.

Thoughts are where change begins. Your thoughts are what set change in motion. Your questions are what set your thoughts in motion. *Magic Questions*® are the easiest way to choose what you think about.

And here's the payoff:

When you can choose your thoughts, you can choose your results

Imagine how different your life might be if you could choose your results!

Well now you can, by choosing what you think about.

To illustrate this, here's a fun little trick. Wherever you are at this moment, ask yourself:

What do I see that is red?

Now look around for a few seconds, paying attention to whatever you see. Then close your eyes. (**Unless you're driving. In that case keep your eyes on the road!**)

As you think about what you just looked at, what did you see that was red? Imagine in your mind's eye whatever you saw that was red.

Open your eyes and ask yourself this:

What do I see that is green?

Look around for a few moments, and then close your eyes. As you think about what you just looked at, what did you see that was green?

Chances are that after the first question you noticed objects that were red and after the second question you noticed objects that were green. You really couldn't help yourself because your questions told your mind what to pay attention to.

Just for fun, you can try this again with different colors.

This simple exercise demonstrates how quickly and dramatically even simple questions can redirect our thoughts, and in doing so determine our results. Just imagine how this plays out in real life.

Have you ever wondered why it's so hard to make a lasting change in your life? It's because we tend to focus on trying to change our behavior, instead of our thinking. That's backwards. You can't change your behavior without first changing the thoughts that give rise to the behavior.

This is the great disconnect between the conventional wisdom about success, and being able to make real changes in real life, the way you can with *Magic Questions*.

Magic Questions help you reconnect the conventional wisdom of success with the real world, so you can make real changes in your career and your life.

Conventional wisdom tends to advise you how to live your life in a certain way. It may be great advice, but to make lasting changes in your life, first you have to change your thoughts. That's what *Magic Questions* do, and they do it better than any other tool on the planet.

We've all heard the ancient Chinese proverb: A journey of a thousand miles begins with a single step. Well, that's the conventional wisdom. But there's more to it than that.

A journey actually begins with a thought. That's the first step of every journey. When you change your thoughts, you change your journey.

But here's the thing: You can't change your journey until you change your thoughts.

That's where *Magic Questions®* work their magic.

Magic Questions give you the almost unbelievable power to change your thoughts at will. If you've never experienced that before, you owe it to yourself to try it, so you see what it feels like to have your own, personal superpower.

If you try to change your behavior without first changing your thoughts, you will fail.

Full Stop.

But if you change your thoughts first, your behavior will follow just like a car moves in the direction you turn the wheels.

Here's what's really amazing about *Magic Questions*: When you change your thoughts, you begin to change your life at the speed of thought.

But there is a catch.

How long any change lasts depends on how long your new thoughts last, and thoughts are fleeting. They're here one moment and gone the next.

To make matters worse, much of what we think about is the result of habit. New thoughts can revert to old thoughts in a heartbeat if you let old habits kick back in.

So here's the tricky part of making changes that last, and it's a problem for which the conventional wisdom about success doesn't have a good solution:

How do I program my brain with the right thoughts when I've spent a lifetime programming it with the wrong thoughts?

The answer is to use the same simple mechanism—questions—that you've been using all along, even if you've never been aware of it.

But now that you are aware of it, you get to choose what you think about, instead of having these choices made for you by subconscious habits or buried memories or the million and one distractions that are desperately vying for your attention every moment of every day.

Now that you're aware of what *Magic Questions* can do, you can use them to instruct your brain what to think about.

Magic Questions are the game changer that can catapult you to a whole new level of success and fulfillment that's a quantum leap beyond anything possible with the conventional wisdom of success.

To change your thoughts, change your questions. The easiest way to do this is to follow *The 10-Second Superpower Secrets*™ you're going to learn in the next chapter. Then keep practicing it with all of the *Magic Questions* that follow.

How to Read This Book

My objective in writing this book is to help you unlock your potential. What is your objective for reading it?

In fact, let's turn this into your first official *Magic Question*:

What do I want to get from this book?

In the next chapter you'll learn a simple strategy for asking questions like this in a way that can supercharge your results.

For now, keep in mind that there are more than 400 of these *Magic Questions* to come. Each one can be a tool to help you make a breakthrough in your work and your life, but pace yourself. Trying to change 400 things at once is a bit much for anyone to handle.

With that in mind, I've organized all these questions into seven books, each with its own theme. As you work from one book to the next, focus on just one question at a time. Take as long as you need to extract as much value as you can from each question. Don't worry about the other 400; they'll be here when you need them.

Begin at the beginning, right here in **BOOK 1: THE 10-SECOND SUPERPOWER**. It consists of nine chapters, including this one. Read the rest of these chapters without asking yourself any more questions. It'll take about 30 minutes. Get the big picture first, then come back to ask yourself the questions.

When you do, take as much time as you need. Each *Magic Question* is a golden opportunity to change your life at the speed of thought. Each brings you one step closer to turning *Magic Questions* into a magic habit.

Do the same thing with the other six books. Read each one straight through to get the big picture. (The average reading time per book is about 45 minutes.) Then come back to ask yourself each question in that book. When you encounter a *Magic Question* that works particularly well for you, copy it down somewhere and file it so you can find it when you need it.

The beauty of a *Magic Question* is that you can never wear it out. You can never ask it too many times. You can never apply it to too many problems, challenges, or opportunities. Whenever you need it you can use it as often as you need it.

When you're finished with all seven books you can use the Table of Contents as a useful resource to navigate back to questions and topics you find especially interesting.

As you move from book to book, think of each *Magic Question* as a portal, a door you can open to a 10-second superpower for your business and your life. When a question really engages you, follow wherever it takes you, for as long as it takes you.

Along the way, the *Magic Questions* you encounter will challenge and stretch you in ways you can't yet imagine. Even better, they'll teach you the habit of asking yourself *Magic Questions*. This is the best thing that can happen to you from reading this book. Imagine a whole lifetime of access to your own, personal, 10-second superpower!

If you choose to make that happen—and it is your choice—then you better buckle your seatbelt, because from that moment on it's going to be an absolutely mind-blowing ride.

2

The 10-Second Superpower
Secrets

*E*ven the simplest question can hijack your thoughts. Like this one:

What color are your mother's eyes?

The wrong question can hijack your life.

Have you ever wondered what happens in our brain when we're asked a question? Even brain scientists don't know. There's evidence that being asked certain types of questions can increase activity in the parts of the brain where we experience pleasure and reward.[1] That doesn't tell us why it happens or what it means; all we know is that it feels good.

There's also evidence that people change their behavior merely from being asked a question about it. In one study, when a group of people were asked if they intended to vote, 25% more of them voted than those in the control group, who hadn't been asked.[2] Another study found that when people in one group were asked if they were going to buy a car, they were 35% more likely to buy a car than were those in a group where no one was asked.[3]

These are significant impacts just from being asked a question, but they still don't give us a clue about what's happening inside the brain, or why.

My own theory is that human beings are a question-based life form. We literally think with questions. When we're asked a question, it creates a vacuum in our mind. Nature abhors a vacuum, so we have trouble thinking about anything else until we come up with an answer or we're asked another question, which yanks our brain in a new direction.

If science can't tell us why any of this happens, let me suggest an entirely unscientific explanation: *some questions are magic*.

If that's a tad too cosmic for you, then how about this:

Some questions produce results that feel like magic

These are the ones we're going to focus on in this book. But what makes them so different from the rest?

Most of the questions we ask are directed at others. *Magic Questions®* are questions we ask ourselves. That's where the magic begins.

To quote psychologist Dr. Robert Karl Guthrie, "Human beings are born to ask questions. *Magic Questions* turn that skill into a superpower."

There's nothing complicated about asking *Magic Questions*. There's no ten-step process to memorize, no checklist to follow, no mantra to chant. The power of a *Magic Question* isn't limited by language, gender, culture, race, education, age, or IQ. Anyone on the planet can ask a *Magic Question* to help solve any problem. All it takes is about 10 seconds to ask it out loud and begin listening to your answers.

Magic Questions are the best tool on the planet to help you choose what you think about. They let you hack directly into your brain to unlock resources you never knew you had to accomplish what you never knew you could. When you combine this with their uncanny power to cut through emotional red tape, *Magic Questions* become the ultimate catalyst for instant transformation.

If you ask yourself the right question, in the right way, at the right time, you change your life at the speed of thought.

But there is a trick to it. The right questions take you where you want to go in life. The wrong questions take you in the opposite direction. The trick is understanding the difference.

3 Magic Principles

The first principle of asking *Magic Questions*® is to understand that you get to choose the questions you ask yourself.

Most of us are blissfully unaware of this. Like so many things in our lives, the questions we ask ourselves tend to flow from habit. We tend to keep asking the same questions we've always asked and keep getting the same results. That's how we get stuck. But we don't have to remain that way.

We can choose to ask ourselves different questions. We can choose to become an active participant in our own life instead of a passive prisoner of old habits. We can choose to ask ourselves questions that take us where we want to go, instead of where we've been.

The second principle is to realize that you have to choose. You cannot escape making a choice. Having the freedom to choose means you no longer have the freedom not to choose.

Either you choose the questions you ask yourself, or you choose not to. Even choosing not to choose is a choice. There are no alternatives. There is no middle ground. There is no one to delegate this to. Like it or not you have to choose, and the choice begins and ends with you.

The third principle is that you can actually learn how to ask yourself the right question, in the right way, at the right time. In fact, it's a skill you were born with, even if you never realized it.

The process of asking and answering questions is how you became who you are. When you were a kid you asked questions about everything. Your entire job description was to fill in the blanks. Through the years, as you began to piece together your model of the world, you had fewer blanks to fill in and asked fewer questions. Questions didn't disappear from your life, but they receded into the background.

What might have disappeared was the feeling of magic that surrounds questions, the sense of an almost mystical power that can summon the resources you need to meet life's challenges and opportunities.

Magic Questions rekindle that power. The same secret that made you who you are can make you who you want to be.

The 10-Second Superpower Secrets™

Most of the of *Magic Questions* in the pages that follow will seem familiar. Don't worry about that. What makes a question magic is not whether you know it, but how you use it.

In fact, most of what you read in this book you've probably seen before in one place or another. What I do is simplify it. I show you how to take the problems, challenges, opportunities, and drama of life and boil them down to their essence, which is this:

> If you want to make the most of your God-given brain, and your God-given life, then learn how to ask yourself the right question, in the right way, at the right time.

Believe it or not, life really is this simple. And the easiest way to find out for yourself is to follow **The 10-Second Superpower Secrets** you're about to learn.

To illustrate how this works, let me ask you a question: *Have you ever been to a cooking class?*

Or a computer class?

Or a golf class?

Or a music class?

Typically, in classes like these you learn something, practice it on the spot, and then afterward you keep practicing it until it becomes part of you. Only then do you really feel like you can cook, or use a computer, or play golf, or play music.

The same applies here. Think of **The 10-Second Superpower**

Secrets as a short class about how to unleash your 10-second superpower.

You're going to learn what *Magic Questions* are, and how to use them. Then you're going to practice this simple skill until you know it.

The rest of this book is more practice, with hundreds of new and life-changing *Magic Questions* along the way.

If you want this new skill to become part of you, simply keep practicing it until it is. The same way you would if you wanted to learn how to use a computer, cook, play golf, play music, or learn any other skill.

If this were a cooking class, for example, we would start with a recipe, and step through it until we created the finished dish.

Later, you could take the same recipe and the same ingredients, and create the same dish on your own. If it's not quite right on your first attempt, then you could try again, and keep trying until you get it right.

Here, we're going to do the same thing. We're going to step through a simple recipe and practice it until you get it right. That's all there is to it.

The good news is that learning how to use *Magic Questions* is a whole lot easier than learning how to cook, or use a computer, or play golf, or play music.

With *Magic Questions* there's only one recipe to learn. Everything else amounts to the raw ingredients. These ingredients consist of the problems, challenges, and opportunities in your life, and the specific *Magic Questions* that can help you with each one.

Learning how to use *Magic Questions* is as easy as falling off a log. In fact, you already know how to do it. You just need to learn how to do it in a way that will supercharge your results.

That's where *The 10-Second Superpower Secrets*™ come in. They're a simple recipe that consists of five almost trivial skills that when used together turn into a superpower. Each of these skills is represented by a letter in the handy little word I use to remember them: **M.A.G.I.C.**

In the previous chapter I told you that I've developed a strategy for how to ask precisely the right question, in precisely the right way, at precisely the right time. Well, this is it.

Pure M.A.G.I.C

The first letter in M.A.G.I.C. stands for **M**aximize your possibilities. You do this by asking an open-ended question instead of a close-ended question.

For example, here's an open-ended question:

What would I like to change about how I do business?

This question commands your brain to explore possibilities. When you ask it properly, ideas start popping into your head.

Here's an example of a close-ended question:

Should I do this?

This question commands your brain to make a decision. Your answer is going to be either a "yes" or a "no" (a "maybe" is the same as a "no" because nothing changes).

When the time comes to make a decision yes-or-no questions can be very helpful, but not when you're exploring options. Not when you're trying to look at the bigger picture. Not when you want to maximize your possibilities.

An open-ended question is thought-provoking. Given that all the outcomes we desire in life begin with what we think about, thought provoking questions come in pretty handy.

By contrast, yes-or-no questions may be useful questions, but they're never going to be *Magic Questions*.

The second letter in the word M.A.G.I.C. reminds you to **A**sk the question out loud, so your brain actually hears it as a question. Believe it or not, when you hear yourself asking a question it's processed by a different region of your brain than if you simply think it or read it. So when you say a *Magic Question* out loud you tell the thinking part of your brain and the hearing part of your brain to work together.

If you want even better results, stand up to ask your *Magic Question* so your whole body feels it as a question.

Your brain and your body are working together every moment of your life, constantly exchanging information and feedback with one another. The more you involve your body in asking a *Magic Question*, the more potent the response you'll get from your brain.

The next letter, **G**, reminds you to **G**rant yourself permission to listen to yourself. Oddly, most of us don't.

When you ask yourself a *Magic Question*, listen to everything your brain is trying to tell you. Even the silly ideas. Even the impossible ideas. At this point, don't judge your thoughts at all, just give yourself permission to think.

Believe it or not, listening to yourself is a life-changing skill. Unfortunately, it's a skill that most of us never develop because we're so busy telling ourselves what won't work that we never listen to what will. As a result, many of our best ideas never see the light of day. What a shame. So don't cheat yourself out of your best thinking. Listen to yourself. If you don't, who will? And why would they bother?

The next letter in M.A.G.I.C. is **I**. This means to **I**nsert yourself into the question.

Most of the questions we ask, we ask of others. One thing that really sets *Magic Questions* apart is that we ask them of ourselves. That's where the magic begins. So insert yourself into your *Magic Questions*, like this:

*How would **I**...?*

*Where can **I**...?*

*What are **my**...?*

Just remember that *Magic Questions* are about what you do, not what anybody else does. That's why you have to insert yourself into every *Magic Question*, or it won't ever be magic.

The final letter, **C**, stands for **C**apture what you come up with.

You already know how important it is to listen to everything your brain gives you when you ask yourself a *Magic Question*, but it's not going to do you much good if you forget your answers.

So capture them. Capture everything. Write it all down. Write it on a piece of paper, or in the notes app on your cell phone or tablet. Write it on a napkin, or the back of your hand if that's all you have.

Don't let anything slip away. *Magic Questions* are so easy to use that you can ask one anywhere at any time. But be prepared to capture your answers, because if you think you're just going to remember them, think again.

Earl Nightingale used to say that an idea is like a fish on a hook. If you don't reel it in when you have the chance, it'll slip off your hook and vanish into the depths.

At first, I didn't believe him because I knew I was smarter than that. But sure enough, one night I had a brainstorm that was so exciting there was no way on earth I could possibly forget it. You know the feeling, like you've just come up with the secret to world peace, or something like that.

Predictably, the next morning my incredibly brilliant idea was gone, vanished like a dream. Have you ever forgotten a dream?

So I learned my lesson the hard way and now I keep a pad of paper on my nightstand, and a pen with a built-in LED that illuminates what I'm writing. I can capture anything that occurs to me, whenever it occurs to me, because I'm not about to let any more big fish slip away.

I can't overstate how important it is to capture useful thoughts and ideas the moment they occur to you. When you ask yourself a *Magic Question* some answers will arrive immediately, but others may appear over a span of days or weeks, and at the strangest times. The brain is funny like that. Sometimes it feels as if the mind has a mind of its own. Our subconscious seems to get a kick out of sharing some of its best work when our conscious mind is distracted. If you've ever had an interesting idea spring to mind when you're taking a shower or otherwise indisposed, then you know what I mean.

My favorite way to capture useful thoughts whenever and wherever they occur to me is through voice recognition. I've been using this technology since the nineties, when it was rough and barely ready, but it keeps getting better. These days I can whip out my cell phone, press a button, and dictate with one hand, while I'm taking a walk along the beach, riding in a car, watching TV, or just about anywhere else.

Except when I'm swimming. I love to swim, for the amazing cardio benefits of course, but also because it's just plain fun to splash around like a kid. There's an indoor competition pool near us where I swim laps year round. And of course, while I'm swimming my subconscious keeps teasing me with interesting ideas when I'm in the water with no practical way to capture them.

But recently I discovered a waterproof smart watch designed for swimming and diving. There were lots of products like that already on the market, but what grabbed my attention about this new watch was that it employs the same voice recognition I use on my cell phone.

So I ordered one on the spot. Now I can capture useful thoughts even when I'm swimming (or in a rainstorm, or in the shower). How great is that?

These practices work for me. What's important is for you to find something that works for you so you're prepared to capture answers whenever they occur to you. If you're just getting started with *Magic Questions*, you might want to download this free PDF:

Magic Answers™

https://www.magicquestions.com/magic-answers-download

Think of it as part crib sheet (stepping you through the *M.A.G.I.C. Model*), and part scratchpad. Whatever you call it, it's a great place to capture the answers you come up with when you ask yourself a *Magic Question*, so you can reflect on them at your leisure when you're done.

Reflect

When you've finished asking yourself a *Magic Question*, listened to all your answers, and captured them, then you can pause to reflect on what you've come up with. You can evaluate which ideas are worth keeping and which aren't. Just don't do that while your brain is still cranking out answers. The minute you start judging what you come up with your brain will cut you off, because it thinks you're done with the thinking process.

Don't sell your brain short.

THERE YOU HAVE IT, ***The 10-Second Superpower Secrets*** in a nutshell. The secrets are simple, straightforward, and incredibly powerful. All you have to do now is practice them. For each *Magic Question* you encounter throughout the rest of this book, keep these secrets in mind.

If you find yourself enjoying this process as much as I do, as well as the new and exciting results you're producing in your life, you might want to check out our game-changing online community of good-hearted people who are creating and sharing the most powerful *Magic Questions* in the world:

The Magic Questions® Goldmine

https://www.magicquestionsgoldmine.com/special-offer-for-readers-of-10ssp

3

If I could change one thing in my life, what would it be?

To see how **The 10-Second Superpower Secrets™** work in practice, let's consider an actual *Magic Question*:

If I could change one thing in my life, what would it be?

Let's start with the first letter in M.A.G.I.C. Do you remember what the "M" stands for?

Maximize the possibilities.

You do that by asking an open-ended question, and that's just what this question is. There aren't any *yes* or *no* answers here. *Magic Questions*® are your opportunity to fill in the blanks in your life with new possibilities.

The **A** stands for **A**sk it out loud so your brain hears it as a question.

So go ahead and ask yourself this question. Ask it out loud. If you're able to stand up, do that, so you can involve your entire body in asking the question and *supercharge* your results.

The **G** stands for grant yourself permission to listen to yourself, to everything your brain has to say.

When you ask this question out loud (and hopefully standing up), listen to the answers that form in your mind. All of them.

The **I** stands for **Insert** yourself into the question. This question is a good example of that.

The **C** stands for capture your answers, on a piece of paper, or your favorite note-taking app, or on a napkin if that's all you've got. Capture everything your brain is trying to give you. Even the dumb stuff. Even the impossible stuff.

Remember, at this point you're just listening and capturing. Now isn't the time to judge, it's the time to write, so keep writing.

Focus on quantity. If you do that, the quality will take care of itself.

If you're just getting started with *Magic Questions*, you might want to download this free PDF I've mentioned before:

Magic Answers™

https://www.magicquestions.com/magic-answers-download

Think of it as part crib sheet and part scratchpad. Whatever you call it, it's a great place to capture the answers you come up with when you ask yourself a *Magic Question*, so you can reflect on them at your leisure when you're done.

After you've finished capturing your thoughts in response to the question you just asked yourself, put your pen down. Stand up and move around a little. Take a couple of deep breaths.

Then come back and take a look at the list of thoughts and ideas you captured.

Now is the time to judge. This is when you reflect on what you've come up with.

Some of what you captured might seem silly. That's okay. Some might seem impossible. That's okay too, because some other ideas you captured might be just the breakthrough you're looking for.

The funny thing about how the brain works is that sometimes you have to wade through the junk until you get to the good stuff. Weird but true.

If you're the kind of person who struggles a bit whenever you put pen to paper, don't sweat it. The best advice I've ever heard about how to cure writers block is to just start writing. Write anything, even if it's gibberish. Don't worry about what you're writing, just write. If you keep writing, you'll eventually get to something worth reading.

The same is true when you ask yourself a *Magic Question*. Start writing whatever comes to mind, even if what you're writing is nonsense. Then keep writing until it isn't.

When you asked yourself the question above, did you come up with more than one answer? Maybe a lot more? That's great! The more the better, because it means you're listening to yourself. Perhaps in a way you never have before.

Asking *"one thing"* questions is fun because there's never just one thing. You can end up making a whole list of things you'd like to change. When you're finished, you get to choose the item on your list that you want to work on first. Later, if other items on your list are important to you, you can tackle them one at a time.

Now ask the same question again, but this time with a twist that might make it the most disruptive question on the planet:

If anything were possible, what is one thing in my life I would change?

Ask it out loud. Stand up if you can. Then listen to your answers—*all of them*—and capture them.

When you're finished, compare these answers with your previous ones. Don't be surprised if there are some differences. We all have an internal editor that monitors what we say and do before we say and do it. Sometimes our editor is so heavy handed it acts as a mental roadblock that doesn't let anything through.

This is common with adults, but not so much with kids. When you ask young children what they want to be when they grow up they give you unfiltered answers: a dancer, an astronaut, a movie star, an insurance salesman. OK, maybe not that last one, but you get the point. Kids haven't filled their subconscious with all sorts of rules and regulations, so they're less inhibited in their thinking. They're at that magical time of life when anything is possible.

Believe it or not, so are we. But a funny thing happens to us on the way to adulthood. As we get a better sense of what we want to do, we also get a better sense of what we think we can't do, and it's often based on faulty information. Then we incorporate our imagined limitations into how we think about ourselves, and accept them as the absolute truth.

For instance, suppose way back in second grade you decided you weren't "creative" because you couldn't draw a cow or a dog as well as some of your classmates did. Kids develop at different speeds, and through the years your talent might well outgrow your misconceptions if you let it. But what many people do after an embarrassing experience like that is to keep telling themselves "I'm not creative" until they begin to believe it. At that point they're effectively imprisoned by this limiting belief for the rest of their lives, unless they do something about it.

If you find yourself imprisoned by limiting beliefs, think of *Magic Questions* as your "Get Out Of Jail Free Card". They can help you reframe such beliefs, or bypass them altogether.

For example, almost any *Magic Question* beginning with "If" or "What if" can help. We'll learn more about how this works in a minute. For now, when you ask yourself a "one thing" question, be sure to follow it up with a version of the same question that begins with this phrase:

"If anything were possible..."

When you ask yourself both versions, and capture what are often very different answers, you get a sense of where you are and where you could be if your limiting beliefs weren't a problem.

When you do this, you might well discover limiting beliefs you don't know you have.

Here are some more "one thing" questions you can ask yourself, followed by the "If anything were possible..." versions. Use these pairs of questions to drill down into areas of your life where limiting beliefs might be sabotaging your success.

Start with this:

If I could change one thing about me, what would it be?

You know the drill, ask it out loud. Listen to your answers, all of them. Capture them.

When you're finished, ask yourself this companion question:

If anything were possible, what's one thing I would change about me?

Like it or not, we are who we are until we choose to be different. It's basic math. If you add to your positive qualities or subtract from your negative ones, the result is a better version of you. "One thing" questions give you the power to do that, one thing at a time.

Here's another:

If I could change one thing about my job, what would it be?

Ask, listen, and capture.

When you're done, ask this version:

If anything were possible, what is one thing I would change about my job?

This one-two punch of asking a "one thing" question and following it up with the "If anything were possible..." version gives you a glimpse of what your internal map of the world thinks you can't do.

I don't know about you, but I grew up with a lot of limiting beliefs, and I finally realized that I've spent too much of my life allowing myself to be body-checked by that kind of nonsense.

These days I prefer to cut to the chase with *Magic Questions* that help me redraw my sense of myself on the fly.

The "one thing" approach can help with anything, including

relationships. Think of a relationship you'd like to enhance. With this in mind ask yourself:

If I could improve one thing about this relationship, what would it be?

Capture whatever your brain gives you, and then ask yourself this version:

If anything were possible, what is one thing I would improve about this relationship?

The "one thing" approach can also help with your health:

If I could improve one thing about my health, what would it be?

Whatever you might be doing to compromise your health, whether it's abusing food or other substances, exercising too little, or not getting enough sleep, chances are it's mostly a matter of habit. Whether your goal is to lose weight, increase your energy, improve your health, or all of the above, *Magic Questions* can help you create new habits that will help you achieve your objective. We'll dive deeper into habits later, but for now ask yourself this followup question:

If anything were possible, what is one thing about my health I would improve?

"One thing" questions can help you delve into the nittiest, grittiest details of your life, like this:

If I could change one thing about my self-image, what would it be?

We expend so much time and energy worrying about what the world thinks of us that we sometimes forget what we think of ourselves, yet this is the core of who we are. There's nothing you can do to guarantee how the world sees you, but how you see yourself is entirely within your control.

Here's the followup version:

If anything were possible, what is one thing I would change about my self image?

Here's a deceptively simple question that can have a major impact on your work and your life:

If I could change one thing about my daily routine, what would it be?

Here's the followup:

If anything were possible, what is one thing I would change about my daily routine?

Here's an intriguing question that might surprise you:

If I could change one thing about my lifestyle, what would it be?

When you're finished, ask this follow up:

If anything were possible, what is one thing would I change about my lifestyle?

Now that you have some experience with this, here's a blockbuster question:

If I could solve one problem in my life, what would it be?

Here's the followup:

If anything were possible, what is one problem in my life I would solve?

No doubt you've heard the old saying that problems are really opportunities in disguise. Here's a question that removes the disguise:

If I could focus on one opportunity in my life, what would it be?

Here's the follow up:

If anything were possible, what is one opportunity I would focus on?

These are only a few examples of "one thing" questions. Any one of them can give you profound new insight into yourself and help you change your life in powerful ways. Allow yourself the time to get the most out of each one that interests you.

When you're done with that, here's a question that can help you discover even more:

What other areas of my life could use a *"one thing" makeover*™?

4

What if I don't know the answer?

---

*R*ecently, I took an online training course on how to use artificial intelligence. I'd been watching this technology from the periphery for awhile, so I decided to take the plunge. (And no, I didn't use AI to create any part of this book.)

As I listened to the instructor, and watched his diagrams and flowcharts, he kept coming back to the same point: With even the most powerful artificial intelligence chatbots, such as ChatGPT, the quality of your answers will never be any better than the questions you ask.

Sound familiar?

He didn't call them questions, of course, he called them *prompts*. But when you strip away the technical jargon, prompts are essentially questions. And the process of asking these questions, what the instructor called *prompt engineering*, is essentially a strategy for asking the right question, in the right way, at the right time.

I had to laugh, because this book is about the same topic. Except that we're not asking questions of artificial intelligence, we're asking questions of human intelligence. Specifically, your brain.

Think *HI* instead of *AI*.

As you learn how to ask questions of the artificial intelligence technologies that are inevitably coming your way, keep in mind that there's an even more important skill to master that's much closer to home: How to ask *yourself* the right question, in the right way, at the right time. And as with AI, the quality of the questions you ask your own human intelligence will determine the quality of the results you get.

In the plainest English possible, the questions you ask yourself— the prompts you engineer for your own brain—will determine the quality of your life.

Consider this example.

From time to time in my seminars and coaching sessions, when clients ask themselves a *Magic Question* the only answer they can come up with is "I don't know" or "I can't think of anything."

They aren't being evasive, and they aren't lying. They really don't know, and they really can't think of anything. Not because they're stupid or incapable of thinking, but because they haven't yet learned how to give themselves permission to think. They haven't yet learned how to ask themselves the right question, in the right way, at the right time. Literally and figuratively, they don't know how to get out of their own way.

They have such an overprotective subconscious mind that it rejects whatever thoughts it deems to be undesirable or unnecessary before the individual becomes consciously aware of them. If they were a brain surgeon in the middle of performing brain surgery that might be a good thing. But what if, after the operation was over, the brain surgeon were to ask, "What's a better way for me to do this procedure to produce better results?" And in response, what if their subconscious made sure that this was the only answer they could come up: "I can't think of anything." In this case, the surgeon, their patients, and medical science would lose all the good that might've been accomplished with some creative thinking, all because the surgeon's subconscious didn't give them permission to think.

Here's a different sort of example. This past Christmas our family played a new game called Blank Slate. We love games, and this one was easy to play, even for those who might have been enjoying too much Christmas cheer.

One person draws a card from a deck and reads the word written on the card. Everybody else writes down the first word that occurs to them in response. That's all there is to it.

Your score is based on how many other people in the room write down the same word you do. For instance, if the word on the card is "dog", you might write down "pound" or "food" or "dachshund". If someone else matches you, both of you get points.

The object of the game is to write down the first thing that comes to mind when you hear the word on the card, and then see if anyone else matches you.

What surprised me was that most of us didn't do that. Instead of writing down the first thing that occurred to us, we thought about it. And then we thought about it some more. We edited our response, sometimes to the point of coming up with no response at all.

Isn't that weird? In a game in which *any* word is an acceptable answer, there were moments when some of us couldn't come up with any answer at all. We were rendered speechless by our subconscious mind working overtime to edit our response.

Whenever that happened, guess what we told the other players?

"I can't think of anything."

Which was absurd, because all we were doing was thinking. But somehow we managed to convince ourselves that wasn't the case.

In a simple party game among friends and family, where there was no wrong answer, it was eye-opening to see how often some of the group struggled to come up with any answer at all, even though *any* answer would have been just fine.

Imagine if this were to happen to you when you asked yourself a *Magic Question*, and the only answers you could come up with were "I don't know" or "I can't think of anything."

If you ever find yourself in this situation, ask yourself this follow-up question:

> If I *did* know, what would I say?

Or this:

> If I *could* think of something, what might it be?

Here's another powerful question that shouldn't surprise you:

> If anything were possible, what would I say?

The next time you ask yourself a *Magic Question,* and your answer is "I don't know," give yourself permission to imagine if you did.

5

What am I going to do about it?

herever you find yourself in life, it's not your fault. It's your questions.

Everything we are to this point in our lives is the result of the questions we've asked ourselves. From this moment on, everything we become will be the result of the questions we ask ourselves going forward.

Questions are how we tell our brain what to think about and what to focus on. The right questions take us where we want to go. The wrong questions can create our own personal hell on earth.

So why would anyone ask the wrong questions?

Two reasons: ignorance and habit.

Most of us never give a second thought to our questions because we don't understand how the brain works. We don't realize that questions are the key to how we think and what we think, and we don't understand that what we think is the key to everything we feel and do.

Remember "the strangest secret"?

In our defense, most of us don't know how a light switch works either. But we don't need to know that in order to turn on a light.

With questions it's different. For one thing, we have a whole lot more riding on them.

Questions are like the ultimate mental light switch. They turn on or off our success, joy, love, happiness, and everything else we want from life. But most of us don't know how to flip the switch.

We tend to have a much better understanding of habits. Habits fill our days. We delegate many of the details and decisions of daily life to habits because they're such a powerful shortcut. When it's time to eat, we don't have to consider all the foods available on planet earth, we just eat what we normally do. When it's time to get dressed we don't contemplate all of the different clothing worn by all the people in the world, we just dress the way we habitually dress. When it's time to watch TV or read a book we don't evaluate every single option available to us, we settle for something out of habit. There's simply no way we could negotiate the complexity of our lives without relying constantly on habits.

But that's also how we get stuck. We keep doing things that are bad for us, long after we realize they're bad for us, because they're a habit. All sorts of activities fall into this category, from substance abuse, to failed relationships, to working in jobs we hate.

Questions also fall into this category. Out of habit, we keep asking ourselves the same old questions that got us where we are, and we keep getting the same old results.

We aren't stupid, we're just human, and humans are creatures of habit. Despite that, we can change. But most of us don't know how.

Chance and Choice

Our lives are the sum total of whatever happens to us by chance and what we choose to do about it. Chance and choice are all we've got.

Unfortunately, there's not much we can do about chance. No matter how loudly we protest the slings and arrows of outrageous fortune, it won't change a thing.

This leaves us with choice. The only way we can make a difference in our lives is to choose to do so. Circumstances may limit our choices, often severely, but they don't eliminate them, and they don't spare us the requirement of choosing how we respond.

Psychologists have all sorts of opinions about when a human being reaches adulthood. I think we become adults when we stop placing blame for where we are in life and take charge of where we want to go. We can't change anything that is beyond our control, but we can change everything else. The questions you ask yourself will focus your attention on one or the other. It's your choice, even when you feel like you have no choice.

In an era defined by crisis, whether natural disasters or man-made, all of which are endlessly reported by the media, it's not unusual for a feeling of helplessness to take over. This is a natural response to a reality that feels out of control. But it's not the only response. Instead, we can ask ourselves this *Magic Question*:

What am I going to do about it?

This simplest of questions can profoundly change your life.

Whatever problem, challenge, or opportunity you have before you, this question lets you shift your thinking into a higher gear. Instead of wallowing in what you can't control, this question gives you laser-like focus on what you can.

Whatever the world throws at you, this question empowers you to choose how you respond. Ask it when you have a problem to solve. Ask it when you encounter an opportunity. Ask it when the world seems to be more than you can handle. Ask it when you feel helpless. Ask it when you can't think of anything else to do.

Ask it out loud, listen to your answers, and capture them.

To supercharge the process, you might want to download this free PDF I've mentioned before:

Magic Answers™

https://www.magicquestions.com/magic-answers-download

Part crib sheet and part scratchpad, it's a great place to capture the answers you come up with when you ask yourself a *Magic Question*, so you can reflect on them at your leisure when you're done.

When you're finished answering this question, reflect on your answers, choose one, and take action.

Do it right now. Every action you take now will make you feel less helpless and more powerful in your own life. You can even turn this into a *Magic Question*:

What action can I take right now to get started?

As mere mortals, we don't get to choose what happens to us in life, but we can choose what we do about it. In this choice lies the difference between helplessness and hope.

Self-Pity

A common byproduct of misfortune is to feel sorry for ourselves. Self-pity is a uniquely human characteristic. As D.H. Lawrence put it in this remarkable little poem:

> I never saw a wild thing
> sorry for itself.
> A small bird will drop frozen dead from a bough
> without ever having felt sorry for itself.
> —D.H. Lawrence

Self-pity is an entirely rational response to a pitiless world, but it's not the only response.

Feel free to marinate in self-pity as long as you feel the need. Sometimes we just have to acknowledge it when life sucks. But when you're ready to choose a different path, ask yourself the question that opens this chapter, a question worth repeating as often as you need it:

What am I going to do about it?

Time and chance happen to us all. Our personal world is constantly being upended and remade, whether from a global crisis or the details and drama of daily living. During this process life has a way of relentlessly eliminating our options. That's the bad news. The good news is that we can create new options. New choices. New beginnings.

The answer to helplessness and self-pity is always the same question, the one above.

Whatever happens to you in life, you're free to choose how you respond. This is the single greatest power you possess.

Magic Questions unlock this power. When you ask yourself the right question, in the right way, at the right time, you really can change your life at the speed of thought, because you change your thoughts.

6

What is my purpose?

*S*ome people are lucky. They know their purpose. They know who they are and what they're meant to do. For the rest of us, sooner or later we're bound to wonder: *"Isn't there more to life?"*

Of course there is. But here's a more useful question:

What more do I want from life?

Give yourself a minute or two to answer this, and another minute to reflect on what you come up with.

Most of us have no trouble supplying surface answers to this question. We want a dream job, better relationships, more money, and a cherry on top. But sooner or later, we realize that even those things aren't enough. We have to dig deeper:

What is my purpose in life?

Ask this out loud, so you hear it as a question. Listen, really listen to what you have to say. Capture everything you come up with.

When it comes to our purpose we seem to have a hidden filter, as if our subconscious won't allow us to consider thoughts that might shake things up too much. Imagine if one moment you were an investment banker and the next you wanted to teach yoga. That would be distracting.

But that's the point. We owe it to ourselves to become distracted by our purpose. Nothing else comes close. Nothing else can give us the life most worth living.

When we wonder if there's more to life what we're looking for is a sense of purpose. As enjoyable as it is to have fine relationships, success in our career, and material prosperity, we human beings want more. We yearn to be part of something greater than ourselves, whether it's a family, a community, an organization, a social revolution, an inflection point in history, or some useful contribution to the greater good. We want life to mean something. Meaning flows from purpose. Until we discover our purpose, we will never really know what we want from life.

If you don't yet know your purpose, your purpose is to discover it.

Here's another *Magic Question* that can help:

What would I like to accomplish with my life?

Take a moment to jot down some answers. Don't judge them; just listen.

When you're done, and only when you're done, ask yourself this:

When I look back on my life, what will I wish I had accomplished?

You know the drill: Ask, listen, capture.

When you finish answering this, compare your two lists. These may seem to be the same question, but they often elicit different answers.

By changing our perspective we can tap into different points of view. When we look forward, we tend to have a shorter time horizon. We may have a clear idea of what we want to accomplish in the next few months or years, but beyond that, not so much. When we look backward, we feel as if we're looking at a much longer timeframe. All bets are off. Who knows what you might be able to accomplish with an entire lifetime at your disposal?

The difference between how you answer the first question and the second is a measure of your uncertainty about what you want from life. When there's no difference between looking forward and backward, you know what you want. You know who you are. You know your purpose, even if you've never called it that before.

Here's another approach:

How would I like to be remembered?

Ask, listen, and capture. This moment can change your life. Give yourself time to take advantage of it.

Now ask yourself this intriguing variation:

If I had to write my own obituary, what would I like it to say?

Go ahead, write your fantasy obituary. There's no better way to understand who you'd like to be than to imagine who you were.

Once you have something on paper, close your eyes and take a few deep breaths. Open them and read what you've written as if you're seeing it for the first time. Read it out loud for good measure.

Does it describe the person you'd like to be?

If so, then ask this incredibly powerful *Magic Question* you already know so well:

What am I going to do about it?

Here's a *Magic Question* to shift your thinking to an entirely new perspective:

If this were the last day of my life, how would I spend it?

This is a great way to cut through the clutter of life and discover what really matters to you. Take as long as you need to capture your answers.

When you're finished, with your list in hand, ask:

How can I fit more of those activities into every day?

When you know what matters to you, you can organize your life around it.

Here's another useful question to discover your purpose:

How can I make the world a better place?

Ask, listen, and capture.

When you're finished, let your answers settle in for a moment. They may surprise you.

To make the world better, you don't have to sell your possessions and give the money to charity; just be your best version of you. Pursue what you're passionate about. Become the person you imagine yourself to be. The human race needs more people like that.

While you're getting to know yourself, here's a question that will rock your world:

What's important to me?

Spend a few minutes with this. Rank your answers in order of their importance to you. You'll be amazed what you learn.

When you're done, and you have a good idea what's important to you, ask:

What do I care about?

Listen to your answers, capture them, and reflect on what you come up with.

Do these last two questions seem to be essentially the same?

Look again. The first one asks for a value judgment. The second asks how you feel. On the one hand you're asking your brain; on the other you're asking your heart. Why not get input from both?

Here's a question that approaches it from an entirely different angle:

What interests me?

If you want to learn something interesting about yourself, make a list of what interests you. Rank it. Let it stare back at you for a moment and sink in.

Self, meet self.

If you were asked to describe yourself, you'd probably respond with something like a Facebook post designed for public consumption. We all want to position ourselves favorably to the rest of the world. Even the obituary you wrote for yourself probably served this purpose.

But in the privacy of your own mind, when you ask yourself what you're interested in, you get a clear picture of who you are. Not who you want to be, not how you want to be perceived, but who you are.

Here's a question that offers an unconventional approach to the process of self discovery:

What do I want to be when I grow up?

Most of us stopped paying attention to this question when the adults in our lives stopped asking us. But it never gets old. In fact, it may be more useful to us now than it was when we were kids because it reminds us we still have room to grow. To paraphrase Robert Frost, we have promises to keep, and choices to make before we sleep.

Have fun with this question. Listen to your answers. Give yourself a chance to reflect. The better you know yourself, the more likely you are to get what you want from life instead of what you don't.

7

What if I could?

*S*ometimes when we're faced with a daunting challenge our first response is: *"I can't do that."* If this happens to you, ask yourself:

But what if I could?

Ask it out loud, so your brain takes it seriously. Stand up so your whole body is involved. Let the question bounce around inside your skull for awhile.

When we tell ourselves that something is impossible, we're lying. We don't know enough to know what's impossible and what isn't.

Before 1954, experts in the medical profession insisted that it was a physical impossibility for a human being to break a four-minute mile. They had reams of data, theories, and explanations to back up their exhaustive analysis of the limitations of the human body. In May of that year Roger Bannister broke through the four-minute barrier for the first time. Since then more than a thousand people have done it, including high school students. The four-minute mile was never impossible, but until that year it just hadn't been done.

When your brain is trying to convince you that you can't do something, don't argue with yourself, just imagine if you could do it. It doesn't cost you anything. It doesn't commit you to anything. It merely gives you permission to think.

Too often, when we think about what is possible in life we filter our thinking with all the imaginary limitations that we've come to accept as truth. We label these as "impossible" and treat them as such.

But *"What if?"* questions allow us to consider these so-called impossibilities hypothetically, and before we know it, they might not feel so impossible.

The *"What if?"* approach to thinking changes everything. It's like playing the old parlor game where someone asks questions like these:

"If you could meet any figure from history, who would it be?

"If you could be any movie star, who would you choose?"

"If you could live anywhere in the world, where would you live?"

The brain at play is a remarkable instrument, capable of so much more than when we encumber it with so-called realities. To get the most from your brain, dispense with all that nonsense being "realistic" and ask *"What if?"* instead.

Whenever you ask yourself a *"What if?"* question, feel free to follow it up with others, like this:

If I could actually do that, what would it feel like?

If you like the feeling, ask:

If I could do that, how would I go about it?

When you were a kid I bet that somewhere along the line somebody told you, "You'd be amazed what you can accomplish when you stop telling yourself you can't." Well, this is your chance.

If you're still stuck, try this variation:

If anything were possible, how would I go about this?

Sound familiar? This is one of the most powerful *"What if?"* questions known to man. From previous messages you already know that it allows us to consider options that might otherwise remain hidden from us. Now you know why.

"If anything were possible…" is a phrase you can add to almost any question and come up with new ideas, new possibilities, and a whole new perspective.

8

What else?

What else?

*C*leanup questions are a special class of followup *Magic Questions* that help you complete the process you begin when you ask yourself a question.

They're important because the brain doesn't always reveal every possible answer when we ask it a question. For example, if someone were to ask you what foods you like, you wouldn't reply with an exhaustive list of everything you've ever eaten and enjoyed. You'd mention a few of your favorites and leave it at that. If the person were then to ask what other foods you like, you'd come up with a few more answers. The two of you could repeat this process for as long as you want, but you'd probably run out of patience before you run out of answers.

When I ask myself cleanup questions, I'm amazed what didn't occur to me the first time around. It's like looking for something you've lost, failing to find it, and then it finally turns up where you hadn't yet looked. Cleanup questions let you keep looking.

Here's the ultimate cleanup question:

What else?

These words can change your life at the speed of thought. Use them, practice them, turn them into a habit.

You can ask this as a standalone question or tack it on to something else.

To illustrate, remember when you asked yourself this *Magic Question* in Chapter 3?

If I could change one thing in my life, what would it be?

Whatever your answers might have been, you can follow up with this question:

What else would I change?

You can dramatically expand your repertoire of "What else?" questions by substituting other key words, including *who, when, where,* and *how.* Put any one of these in front of "else" and watch what happens.

How else...?

Where else...?

When else...?

Who else...?

Here's a hint: There's always something else. You don't know everything. You haven't thought of everything. You never will, so keep thinking.

Let the Air Out of the Tires

The right question can help you discover entirely unexpected ideas. Consider the answers you came up with for any of the questions you asked yourself above. Glance over them. Now ask this:

What haven't I thought of?

If you think this is a "What else?" question in disguise, you're right. Ask it out loud, listen to your answers, and capture them.

When you're done you'll have some new items for your list, items that for one reason or another didn't occur to you the first time around.

If you keep asking yourself this question, you'll probably keep getting new answers that for one reason or another didn't occur to you the second time around, or the third, and so on. Think of it as a general-purpose cleanup question that can help you discover additional answers for any question you ask.

We can never have all the answers, but we can always come up with more. When you think you're finished with a question it never hurts to ask a cleanup question, just to be sure.

Better yet, why not ask your brain to boldly go where no brain has gone before? Consider a change you'd like to make in your work or your life and look at it from an entirely new angle:

What unconventional possibilities haven't I thought of?

Give yourself a minute or two to come up with some answers.

This potent question dares you to think differently than you normally do. It challenges you to consider possibilities you would not normally consider—maybe no one would consider. It gives you permission to imagine the problem from an entirely different point of view.

Albert Einstein is a good example. As a sixteen-year-old boy, he imagined what it would be like to ride alongside a beam of light traveling at the same speed. That shift in perspective contradicted the conventional wisdom of physics. Knowing teenagers, that's probably why it appealed to him.

Within a few years Einstein's thought experiment had evolved into an unconventional solution to the problems presented by the conventional wisdom. He called it the theory of "special relativity".[1] It changed the world.

Sometimes all it takes to solve a problem is to examine it from an unorthodox perspective. I find that fun and exciting. To get in the mood, I like to recall an old story about a tractor-trailer that was wedged under a bridge. Police and firefighters were out in force, trying to figure out how to remove the truck without damaging it or the bridge, but none of them knew what to do. One of the bystanders was a little girl. She tugged at her mother's hand and asked, "Why don't they just let the air out of the tires?"

Whatever answers you come up with when you ask yourself *Magic Questions*, feel free to ask clean up questions. Then, when you've exhausted all the possibilities, ask this:

What else?

9

How can I capture ideas whenever they come to me?

*W*hen you ask yourself a question, you're asking your brain to come up with answers. They may be new ideas, or they may be a new way of looking at old ideas and beliefs.

Whatever they are, when the answers start flowing you have a choice. Either you can listen to what your brain gives you or you can blow it off. But if you blow it off then you're training your brain to stop thinking. Is that really what you want? We humans are prone to some pretty bad habits, but that's about as dysfunctional as it gets.

Assuming you choose to listen to yourself, capturing your thoughts is as important as coming up with them in the first place, because you simply won't remember them unless you write them down.

You already know that I like to capture answers to *Magic Questions* by using voice recognition on my cell phone or smart watch, or with an **LED** pen at my bedside. That works for me, but you need to do whatever works for you.

As I mentioned previously, if you're just getting started with *Magic Questions*, you might want to download this free PDF:

Magic Answers™

https://www.magicquestions.com/magic-answers-download

THINK of it as part crib sheet and part scratchpad. Whatever you call it, it's a great place to capture the answers you come up with when you ask yourself a *Magic Question*, so you can reflect on them at your leisure when you're done.

If you're still trying to figure out what works best for you, turn it into a *Magic Question* and ask yourself:

How can I capture ideas whenever they come to me?

How you answer this might be the most important thing you do today. Ask it out loud, listen to your answers, and capture them.

When you ask yourself a *Magic Question*, including this one, answers will usually begin to appear immediately. But they may keep appearing for hours, maybe days, while your subconscious continues to work the problem. You should expect this, and be ready to capture your ideas at a moment's notice, at any time of the night or day, especially when you're not thinking about the question.

For some reason the brain loves to answer questions about one thing when we're trying to do something else. That's why people so often experience insights while on a walk, or taking a shower, or staring at the ocean. Be prepared for these magical moments. They're your imagination trying to give you a priceless gift.

When you've captured all the ideas you want, that's when you can shift into a different gear and begin to evaluate them. At this point, some of your ideas might seem useless or even silly. So what? They didn't cost you anything. Some of your ideas might seem impossible. Don't fall for that. We already know that's just fear and ignorance talking. "Impossible" ideas are often our best, but we're so quick to dismiss them that we never give them a chance.

Happily, not all your ideas will seem silly or impossible. In the process of sorting through them you may discover a real gem that's exactly what you're looking for. That's why it pays to listen to yourself, and capture everything your imagination has to say.

Book 2: THE MAGIC OF CHANGE

1

How do I create new choices?

*C*hoice is the ultimate survival tool. Other animals are programmed by their instinct to survive. Our instinct is to make choices, and thereby program ourselves. We choose what we do, where we live, who we live with, what we wear, what we feel, what we eat, what we think, and a thousand other details of living. Uniquely it seems, we have been given the luxury of choice.

But nature played a trick on us. In being given the freedom to choose, we've also been forced to choose. Choice is not a luxury at all, it's a requirement of being human. Like it or not, we have no choice but to make choices. Even if we refuse to choose, that too is a choice.

In the seventeenth century, the philosopher Descartes famously declared, "I think therefore I am."[1] As profound as that may be, I prefer to look at life this way:

I think therefore I choose

If you want to change something in your life—or survive change that is forced upon you—you need to make new choices. If you want to make new choices, you need to ask yourself new questions. Choice is the key to change, but questions are the key to choice.

See for yourself. Ask this question:

What would I like to change about my work?

Listen to your answers and capture them, all of them. (Remember **The 10-Second Superpower Secrets™** described in Book 1, Chapter 2.) Take as long as you need. Let your imagination run wild.

Imagination

Speaking of imagination, some people think they don't have any. Ironically, that's a figment of their imagination. The human brain is a volcano of imagination, and that includes your brain. If you've ever had a dream, then you know how true this is. The trick is to harness your imagination in your daily life.

You can begin by admitting that your brain is designed to make stuff up. Imagination is in your DNA. You can't take credit for that, but you can take advantage of it by asking yourself useful questions. When you do, your instinct will take over and fill in the blanks. Call it imagination, creativity, magic, or whatever you like, but your brain is hardwired to answer your questions. All you have to do is ask and listen. The more you practice, the better you'll get. Think of your imagination as a muscle, your mental core. With exercise, your mental core will get stronger. *Magic Questions* are the ideal exercise.

Look at the list of changes you'd like to make in your work. Choose one.

With that in mind, ask yourself:

How can I make this change?

Listen to your answers, capture them, and take a moment to reflect on them.

Then ask:

What would I do first?

Finally, ask this:

What could help me make this change?

Listen to yourself and capture your answers. *Magic Questions* like these can help you come up with new options you weren't aware of before, so you can make new choices. But they also help you exercise your mental core. The more *Magic Questions* you ask and answer, the stronger your core will be.

The Map is Not the Territory

As amazing as the human brain is, in some ways it's too smart for its own good. When we're born, our brain gets right to work building a mental map of our world to better cope with the newness and complexity of this thing called life.

But our mental map is not the actual world, it's just a map. Sometimes we get confused. The map we create can become such an integral part of who we are that it begins to create us.

When I was in sixth grade I struck out on a batting tee. Even for a boy whose body was growing faster than his coordination, this was hard to do. And yes, it was every bit as embarrassing as it sounds. The entire class thought it was hilarious.

Me, not so much. When I swung through that third strike my brain instantly added the experience to my mental map of the world. From that moment on I was convinced that I couldn't hit a baseball to save my soul.

For years I never even bothered to try because my mental map assured me I would fail. It wasn't until high school gym class in my freshman year that I was once again forced to step into the batter's box. I dreaded what I knew was about to happen. If I could strike out on a batting tee, what could I hope to accomplish against a live pitcher?

I knocked his first pitch over the fence.

As I rounded the bases nobody was more surprised than I. My body had grown and changed, but my mental map had not. My hand-eye coordination had finally caught up with my hands and eyes, but nobody bothered to tell my brain. My outdated map of the world still had me believing I was that hapless sixth-grader, flailing away at the batting tee.

I learned the hard way that when your mental map is out of date it's like trying to find your way around New York with a map of Chicago.

A Rose by Any Other Frame

When you want to change something in your life, it helps to update your mental map. *Magic Questions* are a great way to do that. They provide a powerful tool for what psychologists call *reframing*.

The meaning we experience in our lives flows from its emotional and psychological context. When we change the context, we change the meaning.[2]

Remember Rudolph the Red-Nosed Reindeer? At the beginning of the story his nose made him an outcast. At the end of the story his nose made him a hero. The nose didn't change, but the context did. The context in this case was the "frame" in which his nose was evaluated. When the big snow storm hit, the context was reframed, and the meaning of Rudolph's nose was changed, for the benefit of everyone.

Magic Questions are especially good at reframes. Consider a recent misfortune you've experienced. With that in mind, ask yourself:

How might this be good for me?

Give yourself a minute or two to turn this over in your thoughts. Think of Rudolph's nose.

After you've answered this question, ask yourself:

What opportunities exist for me now that didn't exist before?

Change creates opportunity. Even bad changes do.

Suppose you've been fired, for example. That really hurts. Believe me, I know. I've been fired more times than most people have had jobs. But I never got fired from a job I liked. And the traumatic event of being let go gave me the opportunity to find a better job, and I always did.

A *Magic Question* reframe isn't like positive thinking. It doesn't try to make you feel good about something bad. It doesn't try to pretend that you weren't cold-cocked by life. Instead, it acknowledges the pain, and gives your brain permission to explore a new context in which new opportunities might naturally flow from an otherwise negative event.

There's an old saying that whenever the universe closes a door it opens a window. Whenever a door gets closed in my life I think in terms of this *Magic Question*:

What window just opened for me?

2

How do I decide?

*a*s wonderful as it is to have new choices to consider, we still have to decide which ones to pursue. Computers suggest a nifty way to do that, even if you don't know anything about them.

Conventional computers are programmed with a series of binary digits called *bits*. A bit is either a 1 or a 0. It acts like a digital version of an on/off switch. Computers break down even the most complex operations into a series of these simple on/off switches and thereby enable the most sophisticated technology we have, from space travel to genetic engineering.

Binary choices are also a useful way for human beings to make decisions. Our mental processes are more sophisticated than even the most powerful computer, yet we can improve our decision-making by focusing on only two alternatives at a time.

Consider one of the lists of answers you captured in the previous chapter. With that list in hand, follow these steps:

1. Number the items on your list.
2. Compare *Item 1* with *Item 2* by asking: **Which of these two options is the better one?**

3. Take the item you choose and compare it to the next item on your list. Ask the same question.
4. Repeat this process until you've gone through your list.

When you're finished you'll find that something amazing has happened. You've identified the top-ranked item on your list. Based on head-to-head competition with the other items on your list, you've declared one to be the winner. Think of this as your *First Choice*. Write *#1* beside it and set it aside.

Now repeat the process for the other items. Start with the first item remaining on your list and compare it with the second item remaining. Compare the one you prefer with the third item remaining. Do this all the way through the list. When you're done, you will have determined your *Second Choice*. Write *#2* beside it and set it aside. Then repeat the process with the remaining items on your list until you determine your *Third Choice*, and keep repeating this process until you've ranked all the items on your list.

As simple as this process is, it works with any size list for any kind of decision. If it feels familiar, it's how champions get crowned in many tournaments. Competitors pair off in head-to-head competition and the winner moves on to the next round. The process is repeated until there's only one competitor left standing. If it works for Major League Baseball, the NFL, March Madness, and the North American Debating Championship, it will work for you. The more decisions you can reduce to A-to-B comparisons, the easier it is to make choices.

But there's a catch. Even when you narrow down a decision to a comparison between only two items, you still have to decide between them. It may be easy, but what if it's not? Here's a question that gets to the heart of the matter:

Which option do I feel better about?

You've probably been told a thousand times to listen to your gut. This is how you do that.

Here's a variation on the theme:

How does this option make me feel?

If *Option A* leaves you feeling warm and fuzzy all over while *Option B* has you feeling guilty and conflicted, then your unconscious mind is trying to tell you something. Might be a good idea to listen.

Here's a different approach:

If a friend had to make this decision, what would I recommend?

Most of us would rather give advice than follow it. Why not give yourself advice? Pretend you're giving it to someone else. This new point of view might be exactly what you need.

The Truth of Consequences

Decisions have consequences. One way to weigh your options is to weigh their consequences:

If I choose this option, what are the consequences?

When you've answered that question, do the same for the second option. When you're done, compare the consequences of each option and you'll have a clearer idea of how to make a decision.

Our ability to evaluate consequences doesn't come easily; at least not at first. When we're children, we tend to make choices without much thought about consequences. We go to school on a cold day without thinking to take a jacket. We watch TV or play video games instead of doing homework. We're happy to eat hot fudge sundaes and chocolate chip cookies every day.

Growing up is about becoming aware of consequences. If we eat too much, we gain weight. If we don't dress for the weather, we feel miserable. If we choose to play video games or watch TV instead of doing our work, then we fail in school or the workplace. Whatever level of emotional maturity we reach as adults is directly related to our ability to take consequences into account when we make decisions.

Here's a question that takes this maturity to a whole new level:

If I choose this option, what are the unintended consequences?

Every choice we make is a cause that sets in motion effects both large and small. We anticipate some of the effects, but many are unintended. Cause and effect are so complex that we can't know in advance every effect of the causes we set in motion. Yet we'll make better decisions if we attempt to understand their unintended consequences. As the old saying goes: be careful what you wish for because you just might get it.

The Goldilocks Protocol

When we're torn between two choices, sometimes it helps to split the difference. *Choice A* may feel like too much but *Choice B* may feel like too little. The best choice may be somewhere in the middle. Like Goldilocks, we want something that's just right. This is why coffee shops offer drinks in at least three sizes. Too large a dose of caffeine might send you bouncing off the walls. Too small, and it won't get your motor running. But medium, ah, that's perfect.

The Goldilocks Protocol can help with even the most challenging decisions. Consider a relationship you're struggling with. *Option A* is to live with it and accept the status quo. *Option B* is to end it once and for all. But before you resign yourself to one choice or the other, ask this:

What is the middle ground for me?

Listen to your answers. Capture them and reflect on them.

Your answers will depend on the circumstances. If it's a personal relationship, maybe the middle ground is to see a counselor. If it's a professional relationship, you could find someone to serve as your mentor, or someone to act as a referee. In either situation, the middle ground might be to see a little less of the other person, or maybe a little more.

Here's another example. Suppose you're trying to figure out where to live. Should you move to the country, far from your office, to a place where homes cost less but require a longer commute? Or should you move to the city and live nearer to where you work? You'll pay more, but you'll have a shorter commute. In a case like this there is quite literally a middle ground between these options: a location somewhere between the country and the city. That's where suburbs come from.

Or you could try an entirely new wrinkle and think about working from home, even if it means changing jobs. Then your commute no longer matters. This option might never have occurred to you unless you stopped to explore the middle ground.

The Goldilocks Protocol is so useful let's look at one more example. Suppose you're thinking about retirement. If you narrow your choices to only two extremes—work or no work—you may force yourself in a direction you're not ready to go. But if you explore the middle ground, you might discover interesting alternatives you hadn't considered.

For instance, you might work part time. Or maybe you could leave your current job and sell yourself back to your employer as a consultant. You'd be doing the same work, but you'd be working for yourself, calling the shots, and you might make more money.

That feeling alone, of calling your own shots, can extend a career for years without extending the mental grind of working for someone else. Or you might explore an entirely different career. If you've been in the business world, you could turn to public service. If you've been in public service, you could turn to business. Or maybe you could work from home. It's not retirement, but compared to commuting every day it might feel like it.

Despite all the tools we've discussed in this chapter, what if you still can't decide? Try this question:

If I could decide, what would I choose?

"What if" questions have a way of unlocking what's on our mind.

But if you still can't decide between two options, then it really doesn't matter which one you choose, does it? If one choice seems every bit as appealing as the other, then pick one and move on. Or choose to do nothing. It's easy to forget that's also a choice. When you come to a crossroads and can't decide which way to go, then you're choosing to just stand there.

As an alternative, flip a coin. What better way to overcome the inertia of indecision? If a coin flip feels random, it's anything but. The trick is to pay attention to which choice you're subconsciously rooting for while the coin is in the air. That's the one you want, even if it's hard to admit it.

Another way to make up your mind is to ask a more useful question to help you choose. Like this:

Which one can I live without?

Trust your gut. If you still can't decide, choose one anyway and move on. If your gut says you've made the wrong choice, you can switch to the other one and move on for real.

3

What if I can't?

*S*ooner or later when you ask yourself a *Magic Question* your brain will respond with something like this: *What if I don't know the answer?* This is your subconscious telling you to knock on some other door. It's not looking for answers; it's trying to avoid them by filling you with doubt. Shakespeare nailed it when he said, "Our doubts are traitors and make us lose the good we oft might win by fearing to attempt."[1]

In a previous chapter we considered the power of "What if I could?" questions. I call these positive questions. Here we're going to look at their evil twin, negative questions.

For any positive question you ask yourself, your subconscious can deflect it with a negative question. You deal with negative questions by being aware of what's going on, and by continuing to ask yourself positive questions, which are designed to find answers rather than avoid them. Sooner or later your subconscious will take the hint and get with the program.

For example, here's the negative "What if?" question from above:

What if I don't know the answer?

Here's a useful response:

What if I do know the answer?

This is a *Magic Question* literally designed to find answers rather than avoid them. Here's another:

If I knew the answer, what would it be?

Here's one my favorites:

If I weren't afraid to know the answer, what would it be?

Now consider another negative question:

What if it's impossible?

Here's the obvious response:

What if it's possible?

Or this:

If anything were possible, what would I do?

Here's one more negative question to consider:

What if I can't do it?

Here's a useful response:

What if I can do it?

Or this:

If I could do it, how would I go about it?

Positive questions enable change. Negative ones block it. Positive questions expand our possibilities. Negative ones limit them. Positive questions focus on what we can do. Negative ones focus on what we can't.

A positive question takes us where we want to go. A negative question freezes us in place, like a lion's roar freezes a gazelle long enough to kill it. From one moment to the next each of us has the power to choose which kind of questions we ask ourselves.

Choose wisely.

4

What can I live without?

*T*he first time I pruned a rosebush, the process seemed counterintuitive. There I was, butchering a living thing in order to help it thrive. How could that possibly work? Yet thrive it did.

In every life there comes a time for pruning. When we leave behind what we can live without, we make more room for what's important to us, for what we care about, for what interests us. We give ourselves the chance to thrive.

Choose one of the lists you've made about what you want from life. Ask this question about the first item on your list:

Can I live without this?

If the answer is yes, cross off that item and move to the next. Repeat the process for the entire list. When you've jettisoned everything you don't need, you'll finally have time for what you do.

When you ask yourself what you can live without, it helps to ask the mirror-image question:

What can't I live without?

Spend time with this. Listen, capture, and reflect. Decide what isn't negotiable in your life. Everything else is.

Now comes the hard part. Sometimes these decisions are made for us; the pruning happens whether we like it or not.

For example, when the COVID pandemic hit the entire world had to face what it was forced to live without. Billions of people asked themselves questions they never wanted to ask:

- *How can I provide for my family without income?*
- *How can I live without seeing and touching the people I love?*
- *How can I survive?*

Yet even painful questions have answers. They can show us the light at the end of the tunnel.

When you face circumstances beyond your control, let the magic in you shine. Let your brain do what it does best. Ask the hard questions and listen to your answers, even the hard answers. From out of the ashes, create new choices for yourself.

You may be surprised by what you can live without, and value all the more what you can't.

5

How can I turn this into a Magic Question?

agic Questions are like armor-piercing shells that help you penetrate mental obstacles such as complacency, ignorance, fear, and self-doubt. They're usually open-ended questions; you're not looking for a yes or no answer.

For example, instead of a closed-ended question like this—*Is this going to get me the job I want?*—a *Magic Question* is open-ended, like this:

How can I get the job I want?

The first question is binary; it elicits a yes or no answer. The second elicits information and ideas. Yes-or-no questions can paint you into a corner. If the answer is no, it does away with any attempt to find your way to yes, and vice versa.

To be sure, some questions need to be answered with yes or no, or with a binary choice between option A or B. These can be valuable questions, but they aren't *Magic Questions*.

Here's another example. Suppose someone offers you a job. You can ask yourself a binary question like this: "Do I accept this offer or not?" It's an important decision to make, but it's not a *Magic Question*.

On the other hand, *Magic Questions* can help you consider the offer:

What kind of a job do I want?

What do I want to do with my life?

Where do I want to do it?

How can I get a better offer?

Open-ended questions are discovery questions. We use them to learn more about ourselves and discover options. Closed-ended questions are decision questions. We use them to decide between options. Ultimately, we need both types of questions, but our super-power is *Magic Questions*.

When you have a problem to solve, a challenge to confront, or an opportunity to make the most of, ask yourself:

How can I turn this into a *Magic Question*?

For instance, if you need to solve a problem, you could ask:

How can I solve this?

This is an obvious question, but that doesn't make it any less powerful.

There are as many variations as you have time to dream them up, such as:

What is a better way to solve this?

How would I feel if I solved this?

How would my father (or mother, grandparent, coach, mentor, best friend) solve this?

Who can help me solve this?

If I could solve this, how would I go about it?

In like manner, you can frame any challenge as a question:

How can I meet this challenge?

Or:

How can I overcome this?

You can also use any of the variations above and rephrase them for challenges rather than problems.

If you have an opportunity, you can ask:

How can I make the most of this?

Or try the variations above, rephrased for opportunities.

You can even turn the process of asking questions into a question:

What is a useful variation on that question?

What is another question I can ask myself?

What is a good follow up question?

Whatever life throws at you, when you know how to ask *Magic Questions*, you can fill your life with Magic Answers™.

6

What am I afraid of?

illions of years ago our ancestors evolved a life-saving response to the threats they faced in a dangerous world. Respiration accelerated to increase the supply of oxygen. Heart rate and blood pressure increased to direct more blood to the muscles. The brain flooded the bloodstream with chemicals that equipped the body for fight or flight.

This response is still with us today, but the threats have changed. Fear still amps up our bodies for fight or flight the way it did when we had to confront saber-toothed tigers, but it doesn't do us much good in a job interview, speaking in front of a group, facing a difficult decision, or on a date. Our ancient physiological response to what we fear can cause us to overreact—or worse, to avoid situations that frighten us. This is the real problem. Fear can keep you from living the life you dream of; it can even keep you from dreaming it.

There are many levels of fear, from mild anxiety to heart-pounding phobia. Most of our fear, like an iceberg, is below the surface. It grows in dark places, in the cracks and crevices of our subconscious, sabotaging our lives while we remain largely unaware of its presence. That's what gives fear so much power; it's shadowy existence makes it difficult to confront.

The first step in dealing with fear is to get it out in the open. If you feel something holding you back, or making you hesitate, that's a good time to ask:

What am I afraid of?

Listen to what you have to say. Capture it. In the light of day, when a fear stares back at you from a piece of paper or a computer screen, it might not feel so intimidating.

Ask yourself:

What if I weren't afraid?

Try that on for size. Then follow-up with this:

How would I feel if I weren't afraid?

Let yourself dwell on that feeling. If you like it, keep it.

Not all fear disappears when you expose it to sunlight. Some things in life you just have to do scared. That's when it helps to ask this question:

How can I use my fear to do what I'm afraid of?

There's a fine line between fear and excitement. When you feel fear, your body is preparing to fight or run away. Think of all that energy just begging to be used.

Ask yourself:

How can I take advantage of that energy?

You don't have to be an adrenaline junkie to use adrenaline to your advantage. You just have to channel it so it propels you forward instead of backward.

Like this:

How can I use fear to fuel courage?

Courage isn't the absence of fear—it's the willingness to do what you're afraid of. When you commit to that, adrenaline becomes your friend rather than your enemy.

That's why adrenaline junkies do what they do; not because they're tempting fate, but because they've learned that when you act despite your fear, you transform fear into an unbelievable source of energy.

Hard Answers

When we begin asking ourselves *Magic Questions*, we may be afraid to ask the hard questions because we're afraid of hard answers. If that happens to you, ask this:

If I weren't afraid to know the answer, what would I come up with?

You may learn something important about yourself. You may discover options you didn't know you had. Act on them or not, it's up to you. Either way, you're the one making the decision, instead of allowing hidden fears to make it for you.

7

How can I turn Magic Questions into a habit?

*C*ongratulations! You're almost finished with **BOOK 2: THE MAGIC OF CHANGE**. When you're done with this chapter, take a break from learning and focus on doing.

As a matter of fact, while you're shifting into the "doing" phase, I'd like to ask you a favor.

If you're finding this book useful, please post a comment on Amazon. Here's the link:

10-SECOND SUPERPOWER

https://a.co/d/8zdvxov

A review means the world to me as an author, and it's also a great way to spread the word to others who might benefit from this unique book.

If you choose to do so, thank you!

Meanwhile, the best way to transition fully into a "doing" mode is to turn *Magic Questions* into a habit.

To help you with this, ask yourself the obvious question:

How can I turn *Magic Questions* into a habit?

When I was a teenager I wanted to play guitar. I tried to teach myself several times, but each time, after a few days of frustration and sore fingertips, I gave up. When I went to college I shared this story with a musician friend of mine. His response surprised me. "I can teach you how to play guitar in a month," he said, "but if you want me to give you lessons, you have to agree to practice every day, for at least twenty minutes a day, for thirty days in a row. If you miss a day, you have to promise to start over."

This seemed like a dream come true. Only twenty minutes a day to learn how to play guitar!

I took him up on it, and as you might imagine it turned out to be harder than I thought. With a schedule full of classes, studying, and exams, not to mention parties, the twenty minutes a day proved to be more elusive than I had anticipated. Obviously, my friend knew this would be the case, which is why he made me promise to start over if I missed a day. This commitment kept me on the straight and narrow for the full thirty days.

Sure enough, in a month I could play guitar. I was no rock star, but I knew enough chords and finger patterns to play lots of songs. More importantly, I had developed the habit of playing every day. This was the secret, just as my teacher knew it would be.

You can create almost any habit in thirty days if you follow the same guidelines. Practice your new habit for at least twenty minutes a day for thirty days in a row. Think of it as the *20/30 Plan*. If you miss a day, reset the counter to Day 1, and continue for thirty days in a row. Don't just focus on your goal, focus on the new process you're putting place, the changes in your behavior that will become a new habit. That's where the magic happens.

You can do the same thing with *Magic Questions*. For the next thirty days, ask yourself a different question every day. Listen to your answers, capture them, and reflect on what you come up with. If you miss a day, reset the counter to Day 1, and continue for thirty days in a row.

You already have plenty to work with. In these first two books you've encountered dozens of *Magic Questions*. Hundreds more follow.

To get started on your new magic habit choose a question to ask yourself right now. Maybe it's a question you've already found useful (you can reuse *Magic Questions* as often as you want). Or maybe you want to try a new question from the Table of Contents, or a random question from almost any page of this book (where you'll find more than 400 *Magic Questions*).

When you've decided which *Magic Question* to ask yourself today, use **The 10-Second Superpower Secrets™** described in Book 1, Chapter 2 to supercharge your question. Better yet, use the Magic Answers™ PDF you can download for free. It already has **The 10-Second Superpower Secrets™** built into it.

Magic Answers™

https://www.magicquestions.com/magic-answers-download

Then schedule a time tomorrow to ask a different question. To give yourself a head start, choose the question now, and write it on your calendar. Or make it an alarm on your cell phone.

Keep this routine going for thirty days. If you miss a day start over. Reset the counter to Day 1 and continue for thirty days in a row. The key is to do this thirty consecutive days in a row. Before you know it, you'll turn *Magic Questions* into the *Magic Habit*.

Speaking of habits, they tend to be a very popular topic in my training and consulting engagements. If you want to join a community of good-hearted people who are focused on creating and sharing the most powerful *Magic Questions* in the world, and you'd like to participate in monthly *Superpower Coaching™* calls with me, you might want to check this out:

The Magic Questions® Goldmine

https://www.magicquestionsgoldmine.com/special-offer-for-readers-of-10ssp

Book 3: THE MAGIC IN ME

1

How can I cause the effect I desire?

*E*verything we do sets in motion a cause that produces an effect. To get what we want from life, we have only to set in motion the causes that will produce the effects we desire.

Think of something you want to accomplish in your business, your personal life, or your community. With this thought in mind, ask yourself:

What cause can I set in motion to produce the desired effect?

Give yourself a minute or two to come up with ideas.

When you're done, notice that your answers speak to what you *can* do instead of what you *can't*. Our brains have a gift for jumping to conclusions about the road ahead.

This mountain is too high to climb.

This river is too wide to cross.

These obstacles we're facing are too difficult.

But when we think in terms of cause and effect, we change the dynamic. "Can't" becomes irrelevant when we begin with the assumption that we *can*.

Once you throw this switch in your brain, you'll never be powerless again. You'll become a participant in your life instead of a spectator. You'll stack the deck in your favor by focusing your intellect and energy on how to get what you want instead of reasons why you can't.

If at any point you don't like where your life is headed, ask yourself:

What cause can I set in motion that will produce the outcome I desire?

Or this:

How can I change the outcome by changing the cause?

You can combine these two questions into one that is even more powerful:

How can I cause the effect I desire?

This is one of those questions that can be used in almost any situation. Practice it. When you turn it into a habit, you'll be in the driver's seat for the rest of your life.

2

What have I learned from this?

*W*hen he made a mistake, a friend of mine used to say, "I've never had any education I didn't have to pay for." The bigger the mistake, the more he learned from the experience.

Get what you pay for. When you make a mistake, ask yourself:

What have I learned from this?

Just make sure you learn the right lesson instead of the wrong one. Remember the first time you touched a hot stove when you were a kid? Maybe you don't, but your fingers do, and you've tried to avoid that mistake ever since.

But you haven't avoided stoves.

If you want to learn something useful from an experience, add the word "useful" to your *Magic Question*:

What is something useful I can learn from this?

Imagine a life in which in which you can learn from your mistakes the same way you learned not to touch a hot stove. Make it a habit by asking questions like these:

What did I learn that can help me next time?

What did I learn about anticipating problems before they arise?

What did I learn that will make me better at this?

Here's a question that puts a different spin on things:

What do I wish I'd learned before this happened?

We have 20/20 vision in hindsight. Why not turn hindsight into foresight? It's a great way to approach your next project or tackle an obstacle.
So is this:

What do I need to learn about this that I don't yet know?

Making a mistake can teach us a lesson. But what if we could learn the lesson before we make the mistake? It's possible, if we ask the right questions.

3

How would I like to feel right now?

*W*hen we're swept away in a river of negative emotion you might think our first instinct would be to swim ashore. Instead, we often choose to tread water. Emotions have an inertia that defies sober reflection. Like wildfires, they rage until they burn themselves out.

If you'd rather not wait that long, then thenthenyou need to learn how to fight these wildfires. As much time as we spend thinking about the way we feel, we may not realize that we feel the way we think. So the easiest way to feel differently is to think differently. If you want to experience a new emotion, choose a new thought. *Magic Questions* are the easiest way to do this. Here's one that can help:

What color is the ceiling?

What's this got to do with anything? Nothing, and that's the point. If you want to feel differently, think about something else. As a bonus, if you actually do look up you'll access another part of your brain. You can't help but feel differently. Not perfect perhaps, but different.

You can also ask a more direct question:

How would I like to feel right now?

You may not get a clear answer at first because your current emotions might not want to let your attention slip away that easily. You can short-circuit this dynamic by asking:

When this is over, how would I like to feel?

This question acknowledges your negative emotion's right to exist, while giving you permission to think about a more useful emotion, one that you'd like to feel when this particular wildfire is out.

As it happens, our brains can't think of another emotion in any meaningful way without feeling it to some degree. This may be all it takes to break free from the grip of a negative emotion.

Or not. Emotions are stubborn things. Believe it or not, most of the time we want to feel the way we're feeling, even when we feel bad. Why else would legions of moviegoers seek out tearjerkers and horror movies? Because they like crying and they like feeling terrified. Go figure.

This same dynamic is true for all the entertainment we consume: from books, to music, to video games, to sports. There's a reason Shakespeare wrote tragedies as well as comedies, a reason the blues are called the blues, and a reason thrillers are called thrillers. We choose what we read, watch, and listen to as a way of choosing how to feel.

You can use this to your benefit. Next time you want to shift your mood, ask:

What could I watch (or read or listen to) that would put me in a better mood?

Choose something that will help you feel the way you want to feel.

Too often, we do the opposite. We feel lousy so we seek entertainment to reinforce that feeling. There may be a valid reason for doing this. If you recently broke up with someone, for example, you might choose to watch a tragic love story because it makes you feel like you're not alone in your pain.

On the other hand, you could also choose to watch a movie that ends happily. It can give you a sense of hope that you might not otherwise experience in the depths of your despair. Either way, it's your choice.

You can choose what to feel by choosing what to watch, read, or listen to. If you find yourself stuck in a bad place, keep that in mind.

Speaking of being stuck in a bad place, *Magic Questions* can help you fix that when you're ready. Next time you're feeling an emotion you'd rather not feel, ask yourself:

What's the opposite of what I'm feeling?

Just trying to answer this question out can help you feel differently. Then, when you come up with an answer, ask this follow up:

What would that feel like?

Movement

Movement is linked to emotion because our bodies are linked to our brain. When you change how you move you change how you feel. If you want to feel differently, move differently. Turn it into a question:

How can I move differently right now?

Have fun with this. Be creative. Most importantly, move.

If you're sitting, stand up. If you're standing, move around. Try some stretches, or push-ups, or jumping jacks. Dance as if nobody's watching. Do whatever exercise your health and conditioning allow.

Breathing is one of the most effective ways to change what we're feeling. When we're trying to calm someone down, we often say, "Take a deep breath." There's a reason for that. Our bodies and minds are hardwired together. What we do with one affects the other.

For instance, next time you're with a child who's throwing a tantrum, try this experiment. Ask the child to look up at the ceiling and tell you what color it is. (Yep, it's the same question you asked yourself a minute ago.) Whatever answer the child gives you, look up at the ceiling and ask this follow-up question: *Are you sure?* Watch what happens.

Keep this in mind next time you're throwing a tantrum. Our emotions are a function of what's going on in our body and mind. If we change what we're doing with one or the other (or both), we change how we feel. There's no way around it.

Fantasy

If you've ever had a daydream or a fantasy, you know how powerful they can be. They allow us to try out new feelings and new experiences, or relive past ones. We can go places and do things that we might not otherwise be able to do, all without physical risk or expense. Emotionally, our daydreams and fantasies can transport us wherever we want to be. If you're in a bad place, that might be enough to feel better.

Think of fantasizing as a skill that empowers you to choose how you feel. No, you can't snap your fingers and jump from one strong emotion to another. But you can begin the journey by thinking about something else and imagining how it would feel. Before you know it, the stranglehold the negative emotion has on you will be weakened, and a new emotion becomes a possibility.

Here's a *Magic Question* that can help you develop this skill. Next time you're trying to move from a negative emotion to a positive one, imagine where you'd like to end up. With this end-state in mind, ask yourself:

If I could feel that right now, what would it feel like?

Don't be afraid to give your imagination a little help. We experience the world in terms of our five senses: Vision, hearing, touch, smell, and taste. When you want to imagine something in all its glory, fill in the blanks with sensory details. The more detail you can imagine, the more you'll feel. Think of it as your own version of virtual-reality. You get to adjust everything: the location, characters, lighting, colors, sounds, weather, objects around you, tastes and smells, and the feeling of what you're touching.

Once you identify how you'd like to feel, and you've begun to imagine what it would feel like, here's a useful finishing question:

What would help me feel that way?

And this:

How would I begin that?

As you learn how to consciously choose what you feel, keep in mind that emotions serve us in ways we don't always understand. Grief is an example. It can help us remember how much we care for what we've lost. If we could erase the grief, would we even want to? Maybe, in some cases. In others, maybe not.

Emotions are our most authentic selves. We've evolved to be thinking animals, but we're still animals. We're still of this Earth, and emotions are how we feel most grounded.

All of our emotions have their place, but sometimes they wear out their welcome. That's when it's time to move on and change the channel on the movie we're watching in our brain. We can do this by thinking differently, moving in new ways, choosing to watch another channel, and naturally, by asking *Magic Questions*.

4

How can I change my habits?

We face so many decisions each day that we have to rely on mental shortcuts to cope with them. Two of the most useful shortcuts are routines and habits.

Routines allow us to delegate our most common choices to subconscious processing, such as the steps we take to get ready for work in the morning. Each of these steps is something we choose to do, but when we flip the switch to automatic we don't have to make so many conscious decisions, so our cognitive resources are free to think about something else.

As useful as a routine can be, it's nothing more than a sequence of well-rehearsed choices, any one of which we can change. You'd be amazed how refreshing that can feel. Start with something simple, like this:

What's a different way to get to work this morning?

Think about it. Capture a few answers. If you don't have to commute to work then substitute some other routine destination, such as the grocery store or the gym.

It might seem like a small thing, but if you take a different route to a routine destination it will give you new sights and sounds to discover, and the opportunity to think new thoughts. Even if you work from home, you can get to your workspace via a different route than you usually would. Maybe you'll notice something you wouldn't normally notice and think thoughts you wouldn't normally think. If you take the subway, bus, or carpool to work then pay attention to where you're going instead of looking at your phone. Notice what you wouldn't normally notice. When you do it again the next day, see what you missed.

A small change in routine can open your mind to large possibilities. As a bonus, when you make different choices about the least important matters in life, you remind yourself you can make different choices about the most important ones as well.

One easy way to change your routine is to sample something new. For instance, you could ask yourself:

What type of music do I rarely listen to?

Capture a few answers. Then try a new type of music at least once a week. Think of it as a safe way to step outside your comfort zone. You might not like what you hear, or it might become a life-long passion. You can do the same thing with any of these questions:

What news channels do I rarely watch?
What websites do I rarely visit?
What kinds of food do I rarely eat?
What friends do I rarely see?

Sample something new each week. When you do this you return bite-sized chunks of your life to the realm of conscious choice, a skill that empowers you to make new choices in any area of your life.

Habits

Habits are routines on steroids. Like routines, they're a useful way to delegate some of life's recurring choices to the unconscious mind. Unlike routines, habits can assume a life of their own. Before we know it, our habits are no longer working for us; we're working for them. These unconscious choices become so compelling they begin to direct our conscious choices. This is what makes a habit so hard to break; it resists our effort to regain conscious control of our choices. The good news is that once we understand habits as nothing more than preprogrammed choices, we can reprogram them, like the stations on a car radio.

One way to deal with a bad habit is to replace it with a good one. Easier said than done, perhaps, but entirely possible. If there's a habit you'd like to change, this question can get the wheels turning:

What new choice could replace my old habit?

For example, let's say that by habit you grab a bag of cookies in the evening when you're watching TV, but you decide it would be better if you eat an apple instead. At first, choosing the apple might feel weird, even wrong, because the old habit is still telling you what to do. But over time, if you keep choosing the apple instead of the cookies, it will become easier and easier to do. Sooner than you'd think, your new choice will turn into a new habit. At that point, choosing the cookies won't feel right. All you have to do is repeat your new choice until it becomes habit.

We saw this in action in Book 2, Chapter 7: *"How can I turn Magic Questions into a habit?"*. There we explored how to create a new habit in just thirty days. This same process can help you replace any bad habit with a good one. Decide what new choice you'd like to make and practice it every day for thirty days. If you miss a day, start over. After thirty consecutive days of this, you will have substituted your new choice for your old habit. [1]

The trick is to realize that you can make a new choice even when you're in the gravitational pull of your old habit. If you're still feeling the tug of the old habit, ask yourself:

How do I make my new choice right now?

Ask this question automatically every time your old habit tries to kick in.

Some habits are so deeply ingrained they can make you feel as if you have no choice but to give in. If this happens, try a conditional question like this one:

If I could make my new choice right now, how would I go about it?

Good habits can be a powerful tool to help you design the life you choose. Try this *Magic Question* to get started:

What would I like to turn into a habit?

Capture your answers. Reflect on them. Choose one and commit to the thirty-day process. Not only will you create a new habit, but before you know it you'll form one of the most useful habits of all: *The habit of choice.*

Speaking of habits, they tend to be a common topic when I'm showing people how to make the most of *Magic Questions*. If you'd like to join a community of good-hearted people who are focused on creating and sharing the most powerful *Magic Questions* in the world, and have access to our monthly *Superpower Coaching Calls™*, you might want to check this out:

The Magic Questions® Goldmine

https://www.magicquestionsgoldmine.com/special-offer-for-readers-of-10ssp

---

5

What is my opinion?

---

*F*rom social media, to pundits, to the loudmouth in the room, we're inundated with the opinions of others. With so much noise it's easy to adopt an opinion from someone else and treat it as our own. Entire industries exist to help us do precisely this. Business, politics, religion, and other vested interests would like nothing better than to have us think what they tell us to think.

If you prefer to think for yourself, consider one of your strongly held opinions. It might be about politics, religion, brand loyalty, fashion, sports, you name it. Write that opinion down. Then ask yourself:

What do I really know about that?

Listen to your answers. Capture them. Give yourself as much time as you need.

You might know a lot, or you might know a little. Either way, it's useful to get it out in the open so you have an idea of what's behind your opinion.

Now comes the fun part. With the same opinion in mind, ask:

What don't I know about that?

Again, capture whatever you have to say. Give yourself time for this; what you don't know is likely to be far more than what you do.

Take religion, for example. By one estimate there are 4,200 active religions in the world.[1] If you subscribe to any one of them, what do you know about the others? Opinions about religion are among our most cherished. Yet whatever we believe, the majority of our fellow human beings believe something else, and we know next to nothing about what that is or why. Despite that, we tend to feel certain that we're right and they're wrong, or at least they're ignorant about the version of truth we subscribe to.

Opinions about religion may be the most dramatic example, but the same logic holds for everything else we believe. Consider the strongly held opinion you identified above. Whatever it is, billions of people disagree with you. They're as certain that opinion is wrong as you're certain it's right. Let that sink in for a moment, and ask yourself:

What do they know that I don't?

Take as long as you want to listen to your answers. The people who disagree with you have reasons for what they believe, just as you do. Who knows what you might learn from them if you give yourself a chance?

The idea isn't to embarrass ourselves with our own ignorance. Like it or not, we're going to form opinions about things we know little or nothing about. That's human nature. We're going to cling to those opinions as if our lives depended on it. That's also human nature. But are they actually our opinions, or are they spoon fed to us by someone else, for their benefit rather than ours?

Socrates taught us that the unexamined life is not worth living.[2] That's a lot to ponder, so let's pare it down into something more digestible: *The unexamined opinion is not worth having.*

The next time someone offers you their opinion on a matter of importance, ask yourself:

What is my opinion about that?

Then ask this follow-up question:

What do I really think about that?

Ask the other questions above as additional follow-up questions.

If we don't examine our opinions we'll never get to know ourselves. We've been taught to have the courage of our convictions, but are they our convictions or those of someone else? Give yourself the opportunity to find out. As the poet famously said:

> *Who knows what you'll learn about you*
> *When you carefully examine an opinion or two?*

Okay, that was me, but you get the point.

6

How can I invent my own life?

*W*e live our lives partly by design and partly by default. To live by default means we react. Whatever the world gives us, we react the way the world has taught us to react. To live by design is the opposite. Whatever the world gives us, we pause from our reactions long enough to make our own choices.

Consider something you do because you think you have no choice. It can involve anything: a relationship, your career, or whatever you're supposed to do next weekend. Ask yourself:

If it were up to me, what choice would I make?

Two things happen when you ask this question. First, you pause from reacting long enough to give yourself a chance to think. Second, you remind yourself that it's up to you. It's always been up to you. Like Dorothy in the Wizard of Oz, you've had this power all along, though you might not have realized it.

Whatever your internal programming might be, wherever it came from, that's all history now. Whatever has gotten you to this point belongs to your past. All that matters now is what you choose to do in the present. Not because the past is meaningless, but because it's unreachable, untouchable, and unchangeable.

The present is another story. From this point forward, you have the power to choose what you do with every moment as it comes. Welcome home, Dorothy.

You can start with one of the most important questions there is:

How can I invent my own life?

When we're children, we're taught how to behave. As we grow older, we're given increasing responsibility to make our own choices. Yet the world continues to program us with the choices it wants us to make. We're taught that we have free will, but we're discouraged from exercising it. Instead, our parents and teachers want us to do what they tell us to do. Businesses want us to buy their products. Employers want us to do our jobs the way they require it. Religions want us to believe what they tell us to believe. Politicians want us to vote for them.

All these people are coming from their point of view, not yours. It may be possible that they want what's best for you, but they definitely want what's best for them. Not because they have ulterior motives—although some may—but the only person they know what's best for is them. The only point of view any of us can experience authentically is our own. When we try to put ourselves in someone else's place, the best we can manage is to do so from our point of view.

Other people don't have a clue what's best for you, no matter how loudly they insist they do. Only you can decide. You can listen to all of their advice, some of it, or none of it. What you choose to do is entirely up to you.

Once you understand that, you can begin to live your life by design rather than by default. You can choose to act, rather than to react.

Here's a question that can get you started:

What life would I invent for myself?

Listen to what you have to say. No one else on Earth can answer this question for you. Capture your answers. You can keep them in the present tense or imagine the future.

Consider your answers. Whatever they are, here's a follow-up question:

How can I invent that life for myself?

Again, listen to yourself and jot down your answers.

After you've taken a minute or two to reflect on them, ask this:

What advice would I give to someone who wanted to invent that life for themselves?

Sometimes it's easier to listen to our own advice when we think we're giving it to someone else.

Here's a follow-up:

How would it feel to live that life?

To add a twist to any of these questions, substitute "design" for "invent" and see where that takes you. Ask yourself all of these, and capture your answers:

What life would I design for myself?

How can I design that life for myself?

What advice would I give to someone who wanted to design that life for themselves?

Reflect on your answers to all of these questions. What do they teach you about yourself?

Then ask the now-familiar question that makes everything else possible:

What am I going to do about it?

You now have all the ammunition you need to answer this question. The chapters to come will improve your aim.

Book 4: THE MAGIC OF ACTION

1

Where do I begin?

*G*ood questions open the door to good answers. But even with good answers, you still have to do something with them. When you come up with a great idea, you still have to put it into action.

For instance, consider a change you'd like to make in your life. If nothing leaps to mind, ask yourself:

What is the first thing I would change in my life?

Just for fun, go with the first thought that pops in your head. With that in mind, ask yourself:

Where do I begin?

Listen to your answers and capture them.

If it's a big project, you might come up with a series of steps. Prioritize them in terms of which step to do first. When you've settled on one, begin with it—right now—before you do anything else. If it's a significant step, break it into smaller steps, until you come up with one you can do immediately. Then do it.

If it helps, turn it into a question:

What step can I take before I leave this room?

Whatever you come up with, take action right now. *That's* how you begin.

Inertia

Inertia is a law of physics. A body at rest tends to stay at rest unless acted upon by an external force. A body in motion tends to stay in motion unless acted upon by an external force.

Something similar applies with human behavior. You're a body at rest until you decide to set yourself in motion, and vice versa. This psychological inertia is every bit as immutable as physical inertia. No wonder it's so easy for us to get stuck.

But there is a crucial difference. With physical inertia, a body remains at rest or in motion until acted upon by an external force. With psychological inertia, the force has to be internal. It has to come from within us. We have to choose to take action, because the action we want won't happen on its own.

This is why it's so important to begin right here, right now. Whatever first step you've identified to create the change you want to make in your life, begin that step now. The quicker you turn yourself into a body in motion, the sooner your momentum will help you stay in motion. But only if you get the party started. That's how to make inertia work for you.

The alternative is procrastination. That's how to make inertia work against you. It's so easy to remain a body at rest by putting something off until tomorrow that tomorrow never comes.

If you procrastinate, here's a question that can help you use procrastination to your advantage:

How can I put off procrastinating?

After you've finished the first step you identified above, and you've become a body in motion, then you can ask one of the most useful of all *Magic Questions*:

What do I do next?

Then do it. Turn your thoughts into action. As important as good thoughts are, they're only theory. Change won't happen until you put that theory into practice. The only way to become a body in motion is to take action.

For instance, suppose the change you've decided to make is to get into better shape. That's a wonderful objective because it affects so much else in your life, from your energy, to your self-confidence. But depending on what condition you're in, to get in shape may be a significant project that consists of many smaller steps. To identify what those steps might be, you can ask yourself:

How do I get in shape?

Ultimately, you'll want to create a plan of action to take you from where you are to where you want to be. But for now, the trick is to get started. You need to identify one step you can begin before you leave this room, and then do it.

You might do some stretching exercises, for example, if you're physically capable of doing so, or read a chapter or two in that book about nutrition you've been meaning to read, or search the web for advice about how to get in shape. Each of these actions will turn you from a body at rest into a body in motion. Your momentum will help you stay in motion.

Begin With The End in Mind

One of the basic principles of planning is to begin with the end in mind. For our example of getting in shape, maybe there's a certain weight you'd like to obtain, or a dress size or waist size you're shooting for, or an endurance goal you'd like to achieve. You can figure it out in advance with a question like this:

What do I want to accomplish?

And this:

How will I know when I'm done?

And this powerful variation:

What will success look like?

Here's another useful question:

What new habits will help me keep my momentum?

Once you're a body in motion, you want to stay in motion until you reach your objective. Habits are a great way to do that.

Whatever change you've decided to make in your life, begin it now. Begin with your end in mind. Identify an action you can take before you leave this room, and then do it. Right now.

Then let yourself enjoy the elation of becoming a body in motion, and the thrill of remaining in motion until you get what you want.

So congratulations! You got started!

2

How do I finish?

*S*ome years ago I attended a training session on how we communicate with ourselves about fears and limitations. For one of our exercises each of us had to climb a telephone pole, stand on top, and jump to a trapeze. What could possibly go wrong?

So I decided to increase the degree of difficulty. I had recently watched the movie *Karate Kid*, and naturally I felt like it made perfect sense to climb the pole, stand on one leg in the "crane" position, and execute the snap kick I'd seen the kid do in the movie.

I visualized everything in advance, down to the tiniest detail. Or at least I thought I did.

When it was my turn, I did exactly what I had visualized. I climbed the rungs, higher and higher until I was 35 feet above the California desert. Then I stood on top of the pole, slowly raised my leg just like in the movie, and with my hands hovering menacingly over my head—just like in the movie—I executed the kick I had so carefully visualized. Perfect! I felt like I was on top of the world.

Exhilarated, I leaped through the air with the greatest of ease and grabbed the bar that was dangling a few feet in front of me. As my body swung out into space, my weight suddenly became unbearable, and before I realized what was happening my hands were ripped from the bar and I fell.

I was wearing a safety harness, so falling was no big deal. But I felt terrible because I had failed. I had planned for everything except the finish. The climb, the crane kick atop the telephone poll, and the leap for the bar. But it never occurred to me that the force of gravity as I swung forward would require me to grip the bar far more tightly than I did.

As they lowered me to the ground, I wondered:

What can I learn from this?

The answer was as obvious as it was profound: *Plan your finish.* It's a lesson that has served me well ever since.

Consider something you have to do that will test you in unanticipated ways. With this in mind, ask yourself:

How do I finish?

Think it through. With your finish in mind, ask:

What will it feel like?

Allow yourself to experience the feeling in advance. Then ask:

What is likely to be the greatest challenge?

With that in mind, ask:

How will I prepare for this challenge?

If you believe, as I do, that much of luck is what happens when preparation meets opportunity, you'll do yourself a favor and ask questions that help you prepare not just to begin, but to finish as well.

3

How can I change my habits?

---

*W*hen we come into this world, our full-time job is to learn. We have to learn how to talk, walk, read, write, do math, use the toilet, interact with our fellow human beings, and a thousand other things along the way. These accomplishments seem so remarkable, and come at such an early age, that they give rise to the myth that we have a greater capacity to learn as children than we do as adults.

The opposite is true.

Children are a blank slate. They start from scratch so they have no choice but to learn.

Adults are different. We can choose to learn or not. If we choose to learn, our knowledge and experience give us a greater capacity to learn than we had as children, because we have so much more to build on. The more we learn, the more we can learn.

However, we do face a challenge as adults we didn't face as kids. We don't just have to learn—we have to unlearn. New knowledge often comes at the expense of existing knowledge, which is deeply entrenched in our memory. New skills frequently require the unlearning of old skills. This can be intimidating, especially for people who fear change.

But change is here whether we like it or not. According to a recent study, the half-life of a job skill today is about five years.[1] This means if you want to hold on to your job, you need to be in a constant state of renewal. You have to learn new skills and update old ones just to keep up with changes in the workplace. This may seem like a daunting prospect, especially if you've convinced yourself you can't learn. If you have, then that's the first thing you have to unlearn.

Here's a *Magic Question* that can help. With an obsolete skill in mind (or an obsolete belief), ask yourself:

How can I unlearn that?

As adults we can learn anything we put our mind to, at any age. And we're lucky enough to live in the golden age of online learning. To learn almost anything, all we have to do is consult the Internet. Want to know the annual rainfall in Patagonia? Somewhere between 200 and 400 mm a year, according to Alexa. Finding this answer took me all of three seconds. Want a degree in meteorology? Google tells me how I can earn a degree online, or where I can study at brick-and-mortar campuses across the country. Want to catch up on the latest research on climate change? Siri points me to dozens of resources, from news outlets to academic journals.

Sure, when you're consulting the Internet you have to take things with a grain of salt, and cross check your sources to make sure you're not scarfing up someone else's BS, but the Internet makes it easy to validate information and facts. (I just wish more people would bother to do so.)

We can also ask our human friends, including our extended family of contacts on social media sites that span the globe. The range of knowledge available from other human beings who make themselves and their expertise available online is staggering. For free or for a fee you can find providers of high-quality learning in any subject you can imagine.

Like *Magic Questions*, for example. In *The Magic Questions® Goldmine* you'll find an online learning experience unlike anything you've ever seen before. Every other month there's a *Magic Questions Master Class* where we do a deep dive in how to supercharge your *Magic Questions* to produce extraordinary results in specific areas of your life, such as your business, your relationships, your wealth, and your community. There's a members-only *Magic Questions® Podcast* that is essentially a mini-training every week. And each month we have a *Superpower Coaching™ Call*, hosted by me. You can learn more here:

The Magic Questions® Goldmine

https://www.magicquestionsgoldmine.com/special-offer-for-readers-of-10ssp

Whatever you want to learn, it's easier today than ever before, which is fortunate because as change accelerates our need to learn accelerates.

You can get the ball rolling with this *Magic Question*:

What do I want to learn?

Listen to your answers. Give yourself a minute or two. Capture and reflect on them. Then ask this follow-up question:

If I could learn one new skill, what would it be?

Let your imagination have fun. Capture whatever pops into your mind. Maybe there's a new skill you need to acquire for your business, or a new app to master on your phone. Maybe you'd like to learn how to cook a dish you tried at a local restaurant, or manage your finances, or repair a leaky faucet, or learn how to play the guitar. Settle on something you'd like to learn, and ask yourself:

How do I learn that?

By now you've learned the drill. Listen to your answers. Capture them. Reflect. Spend a moment to put together a list of steps to learn whatever it is you want to learn.

I'm a very lucky person because I love to learn. In the past few years I've learned so much more than I ever learned in all my years of formal education that I'm a very different person now than I was then.

Whenever I want to learn something new, large or small, I start with the Internet and enter a query that is essentially a *Magic Question*:

How do I learn to _____?

Try this yourself. Fill in the blank with whatever you want to learn how to do, such how to market your business, repair a toaster, cook prime rib, or learn calculus.

For example, I've been a photographer since I was six. Not long ago I invested in a new camera that was highly optimized to take pictures of birds in flight, one of my favorite subjects (and hard to get right). As complex as the new camera was, the documentation that came with it barely scratched the surface. I had a choice. I could figure out how to use it on my own or learn from someone who already had.

I decided to put a *Magic Question* to the internet:

How do I take pictures of birds in flight with this camera?

Seconds later I was viewing a video posted by a professional photographer who showed me how to do exactly what I wanted to do with my new camera. I would have paid to watch his tutorial, but it didn't cost me a dime. (I did buy one of his books because I like to support people who support me.) A few hours later I was taking pictures I could have only dreamed about the day before. A year after that the same virtual mentor offered a much deeper dive into the same topic, for a very reasonable fee. Again, it was exactly what I wanted to learn, with the same camera I was using, and the same lenses. I happily paid the fee, inhaled this guy's training, and quickly improved my birds-in-flight photography.

Some people are intimidated by learning something new or unlearning something old. If this describes you, ask yourself:

How can I fall in love with learning again?

The word "again" is important here. We're born to learn. When we were kids, learning was fun. It was all about exploration and discovery. Then we were plopped down in a chair in a classroom and told to pay attention. What had been fun began to feel tedious and boring. Even then, a quality teacher could inspire us to learn. The good news is that with all the resources available online today, excellent teachers and the joy of learning are only a few clicks away.

Think of something you need to learn, and ask yourself:

What if I *could* learn that?

Give yourself a minute or two to consider it, then ask this follow-up question:

If I could learn it, how would I go about it?

Capture some answers, and ask yourself:

If I did learn it, how would I feel?

In this golden age of online learning, we have a golden opportunity to become hello happy birthday buddy lifelong learners—but only if we allow it to happen.

4

What motivates me?

*M*otivation is a tricky thing. Sometimes we need a carrot; other times a stick. Sometimes we need both. To make it even more interesting, our motivation can change with context. What motivates us to get out of bed in the morning might not motivate us to do our taxes, just as what motivates us to learn a new video game might not inspire us to learn a new language. What motivates us when we're in a good mood won't necessarily motivate us when we're in a lousy one.

Think of something you want to change in your life. With this in mind, ask yourself:

What would motivate me to do that?

Capture whatever pops into your mind. If you have all the motivation you need for this objective, then consider a different one, and ask the same question.

When you're finished, ask this variation:

What would make this change worthwhile for me?

Your answers to these questions tell you something useful about yourself. Not only about what motivates you, but about how badly you want to be motivated. Not all change is worth the effort. To see something through to the end you not only have to commit, but it has to be worth it. Otherwise, there's no reason to follow through.

With the same objective for change in mind, ask this:

What makes this worth doing for me?

The greater the difficulty of the change you have in mind, the more certain you need to be that it's worth it. For instance, I'd love to play lead guitar in a rock band, but not enough to practice eight hours a day, give up everything else I could be doing during that time, and spend my life on the road. Even if I had the talent, it wouldn't be worth it for me.

Here's a question that will help you understand the kind of commitment you're asking yourself to make:

What price will I have to pay to make this change?

When you've tackled that, ask this follow up question:

What will I have to give up to make that change?

To get what we want from life, we often have to give up something we want less. The better we understand this trade off, the more clearly we can understand the commitment it requires.

Here's a question that can help:

What will I have to sacrifice to make this change?

Opportunity Cost

If you've ever taken a class in economics, you've encountered the notion of *opportunity cost*. The time and money you commit to one course of action is no longer available for any other course of action. The true cost of one action includes the cost of not doing others.

For instance, if you choose to go to a movie on Saturday night, then you're giving up all the other things you might have done, such as going to a party, a ball game, a concert, or spending a quiet evening at home.

Every choice we make comes with an opportunity cost, whether we're aware of it or not. If we choose to invest time and resources in one activity, then we're choosing not to invest those in any other activity. Our choices have consequences not only from what we do, but from what we choose not to do. If you want to see something through, it's good to understand your opportunity cost going in.

This *Magic Question* can help:

What is my opportunity cost for doing this?

Once you have a clear sense of what making a change will cost you in terms of time, resources, sacrifice, and opportunity cost, then you're in a position to ask:

Is doing this worth the price I have to pay?

If it is, you're all set. If it's not, then focus on what is worth it.

Motivation is not about tricking yourself into working harder, it's about knowing yourself. It's about knowing what's required of you to get where you want to go, and whether it's worth it to undertake the heavy lifting necessary to get there. If it's not, then all the motivation in the world probably won't work.

Think of it as the difference between *willpower* and *why-power*. Willpower is a blunt instrument. You can force yourself to do some things some of the time, but you can't force yourself to do all things all of the time. But when you understand why you're doing something, and why it's worth doing, and why you would rather do it than not do it, then you have why-power. With enough why-power, motivation and willpower will take care of themselves.

Here are three *Magic Questions* that can help you figure this out. Think of something do you want to motivate yourself to do. With this in mind, ask yourself:

Why is this worth doing?

Here's a useful variation:

What makes this worth doing?

Listen, capture your thoughts, and reflect on what you come up with.

Here's finishing question that can help you make your why-power crystal clear:

Why is this so important for me to do?

Intrinsic Value

Some things we do because we enjoy them. We would do them for free. Others we do because they're a means to an end.

To better understand the difference, ask yourself this *Magic Question*:

What do I genuinely enjoy doing?

Take at least a couple of minutes for this one. Give your mind the freedom to roam.

When you're done, think of something you've decided that you have to do, and the price you have to pay to do it.

Do you notice a difference between this task you've assigned yourself and the items on the list of things you genuinely enjoy doing?

There's a difference between doing something because you

enjoy it, and doing something because it leads to something else. The former is *intrinsically* valuable. You do it because it feels good. It's an end in itself. The latter is *extrinsically* valuable. It's a means to an end, not an end in itself. You do it not because you want to do the work, but because you want the results.

When we're working to make a meaningful change in our lives, we spend a lot of time doing extrinsically valuable tasks. We aren't doing them because we enjoy them; we're doing them because they lead to something else. They aren't ends in themselves, they're means to an end. Imagine how much easier it would be if some of these means to an end included things you enjoy doing.

One way to motivate yourself is to incorporate intrinsically valuable activities into your extrinsically valuable tasks. The more you can incorporate what you like to do in what you have to do, the more motivated you'll be to do it.

You can turn it into a *Magic Question*:

How can I include more of what I enjoy doing in what I have to do?

For instance, I've spent much of my life in front of a computer. Through the years I've devoted so much time to pointing, clicking, and waiting for something to happen that I finally realized I could make my workday more enjoyable and more productive if I invested in a faster computer. At the time, the computer I had worked fine. The frugal part of my brain told the fun-loving part of my brain that it would be a waste of money to get a new computer. But I threw financial caution to the wind, and bought the fastest computer I could find, with the nicest screen.

What a difference it made! I couldn't wait to start work in the morning. Naturally, I spent more time working because it felt less like work. The net result was that I added an extra hour of productivity to every workday, not because I forced myself to, not because I felt more motivated, but because the work I was doing felt more like play. I was able to spend more of each workday genuinely enjoying what I was doing. As a bonus, my increased productivity paid for the new computer in a matter of weeks.

Along those lines, here's a question you might find useful:

What can I do that would help me enjoy my work more?

In my example, the sheer joy of driving a faster computer with a bigger and better screen enticed me into working more, and enjoying the whole day more. I didn't need more motivation, I needed more fun. And I got it.

What motivates you? You're the only one who can answer that. You're the only one who knows what makes you tick.

Here's a question that can help you figure it out:

What do I look forward to?

Here's a useful follow-up:

What gets me excited?

Whatever your answers are to these questions, the more of it you can inject into your work, the less it will feel like work.

Incentives

If you've ever received a performance-based incentive at work, you understand how powerful it can be. Why not use the same psychology on yourself?

Go back to the change you identified at the beginning of this chapter. Presumably, the ultimate payoff is worth the price. But if it's a demanding project or involves doing things you don't like doing, it can't hurt to sweeten the pot.

What incentive can I offer myself to do that?

Think of incentives as a reward for doing what you commit to doing. But make sure you don't offer yourself incentives that cause you to backslide. For example, if you're trying to lose ten pounds during the next two months, it doesn't make sense to reward yourself with a chocolate sundae when you reach your goal. Instead, a new outfit or a new toy might be a good idea—or a day off where you do nothing but what you enjoy. Imagine a whole day filled with activities that are ends in themselves.

You'll get the most bang for your buck if you pick an incentive that contributes to your objective. Suppose, for instance, that your objective is to increase endurance in your exercise of choice. One incentive you could offer yourself when you reach a specific milestone is to get some new exercise equipment, or upgrade your gym membership, or invest in a new watch that automatically measures your heartbeat. Not only will it give you a little extra incentive to reach your initial milestone, but it will serve as a tool to help you accomplish the next milestone. It's like earning compound interest on motivation.

5

What do I risk if I don't try?

$\mathcal{N}$o one likes to fail, although failing is how we've accomplished most of what we've done in life. When we were youngsters we didn't just start walking; we had to fall down a lot until we got it right. We didn't just start talking; we had to learn how to speak poorly before we could speak well. We didn't just start reading; we began by misreading and mispronouncing until we learned how to do it right. This process of trial and error is what made us who we are. It can also make us who we want to be, as long as we're willing to keep trying new things, and keep learning from our mistakes.

Yet some people dread failure so much they refuse to risk it. They settle into a comfort zone where there's no trial and error, no learning, and no growth. They think they're avoiding risk, but all they're avoiding is life.

There's a better way. Learn to take reasonable risks. This starts by asking reasonable questions.

Suppose, for example, that you want a promotion. You might ask yourself:

What are the risks of pursuing that?

One obvious risk is that you might fail to get the promotion. If this bothers you, ask:

Is it worth the risk?

If your answer is yes, then it would be reasonable to take the risk. If your answer is no, then ask this now-familiar question:

What am I afraid of?

Listen to yourself and capture your answers. It's hard to break out of your comfort zone if you have no idea what's keeping you there, so it helps to get it out in the open.

Some people are afraid of success. In our example above, if you get a promotion it might mean you have to work longer hours. You might have to learn new skills, or speak more often in front of a group. You might have to relocate. You might even have to update your self-image to accommodate the new, more successful you.

For each fear you uncover, ask yourself:

Is the promotion worth that risk?

If it is, move on to the next fear. If it's not worth the risk, then ask a follow-up question that can help you get to the bottom of things:

What am I really afraid of?

Fears often masquerade as something else: An obstacle that seems too large to overcome, a sacrifice that seems too great, or a violation of a personal standard we've assumed for ourselves. But beneath the surface is good old-fashioned fear.

When we face our fear in the light of day, acknowledge it, intelligently evaluate the risk, and commit to taking the risk despite our fear, then we feel unstoppable, even if we're still afraid. Courage isn't the absence of fear, it's doing what we're afraid of.

When we evaluate the risk of doing something, we often ignore one of the most important factors of all:

What do I risk if I don't try?

In the previous chapter we considered the opportunity cost of making a choice. We should also consider the opportunity cost of not making that choice. When we're deciding whether to do something or not, we owe it to ourselves to understand the true cost of both.

In our "promotion" example above, if all we evaluate is the risk of going after the promotion, that's only half the story. Here's a question for the other half:

What's do I risk if I don't go after the promotion?

This question might lead to others that fill in important blanks, such as:

What's the risk of losing that extra income?

What's the risk to my career if I don't move up that next rung on the ladder?

What's the risk if I don't get to work with the people I might have worked with?

What's the risk if I don't allow myself to stretch and grow in this new direction?

What's the risk if I don't add this to my resume?

When you evaluate the risk of making a meaningful change in your life, do yourself a favor and also consider the risks of not doing it. It may not change your mind, but at least you'll understand what you're missing. Then the choice belongs to you, rather than to a suffocating fear lurking in the darkness.

6

What will I wish I had done differently?

---

*J*n *A Christmas Carol,* by Charles Dickens, Scrooge was haunted by three ghosts, but the one that really shook him up was "The Ghost of Christmas Yet to Come." Scrooge took one look at what the future had in store for him and changed.

We can learn from his lesson. We can't change the past, but we can change the future by what we do right now. We can take a long hard look at where we're going, and if we don't like what we see, we can make changes today that will change our tomorrows.

Here's a question that can help:

Tomorrow, what will I wish I'd done yesterday?

Capture your thoughts and give yourself time to reflect on them.

When you're finished, here's a more pointed version:

Tomorrow, what will I regret having done today?

Or look at the other side of the coin:

Tomorrow, what will I regret not having done today?

Shift the timeframe by asking:

Next year, what will I regret having done this year?

And this:

Next year, what will I regret not having done this year?

Regret is a powerful emotion. Why not put it to good use?

Now imagine yourself twenty years in the future, looking back on this part of your life. Ask yourself:

What do I wish I'd done differently?

Spend some time with this. Listen to yourself and reflect. Whatever your imaginary future may hold, it's not too late to change it by making different choices now.

Ellis's Law

When I was in second grade my teacher tried to help the class understand the value of compound interest. The first step was to put our pennies into a savings account. Like most kids, I preferred to invest my pennies in candy and ice cream, where they belonged. Predictably, years later I did the math and realized how much money I would've had if only I'd listened to what Mrs. Miller had tried to teach me.

The more I thought about it, the more fascinated I became with the principle of compounding, not only because it made money grow like magic, but because it seemed to touch everything in life. Compounding is how we make time work for us instead of against us. It may not seem like a magic bullet, but it's the closest thing I've ever found.

When we take action every day, even something small, over time these efforts compound themselves. The results accumulate by building on prior results. When you stir in enough of the magic ingredient—*time*—you can accomplish almost anything. This notion became what I call *Ellis's Law*:

Over time, even ordinary efforts yield extraordinary results.

I don't call this *Ellis's Law* because I invented it, but because it all but invented me. When I finally understood the implications, it transformed my life.

Ellis's Law applies to everything we do. Given enough time, even our smallest actions become hugely significant. Anyone who has gained weight can attest to that. Nobody sets out to add inches to their waistline or hips, but a glass of wine here, a hot fudge sundae there, and before you know it, you've produced an extraordinary result that stares back at you in the mirror. You might not like what you see, but it's proof positive that even small efforts, over time, produce big results. Once you understand that, you can begin to make time work for you instead of against you.

7

What could go right?

*F*or many of us, when we face something new or challenging, our first thoughts are about what could go wrong. That's a valid concern. If you're learning to skateboard, it's not unreasonable to think about falling, which you undoubtedly will do. But it's equally valid—and far more useful—to focus on what could go right.

When we imagine doing something, we tend to do what we're visualizing because the brain is wired that way. When we imagine what we don't want to happen, we're unintentionally giving our brain instructions to make it happen. We're far more likely to succeed if we think about succeeding then we are if we think about what could go wrong.

Consider something you're worried about doing. Maybe it's taking a test, or speaking in front of a group, or asking someone out. Instead of thinking about everything that could go wrong, ask yourself:

What could go right?

Let yourself imagine that. Allow yourself to dwell on it for a minute or two. Congratulations, you've just increased your odds for success.

Take public speaking, for example. Many people fear it. They can't stop thinking about what could go wrong. They're afraid they might make a fool out of themselves, or forget what they're supposed to say, or step off the podium in the wrong direction and fall down. Okay, maybe that last one is just me. I actually did that once—in church.

When you're preparing to speak in front of a group, whatever you're afraid might happen might actually happen. Or might not. You get to choose which set of possibilities to focus on. No matter which outcome you visualize, you increase the chances it will occur.

No wonder so many athletes practice visualization. Basketball players shoot thousands of foul shots in practice, but they also practice in their mind's eye by visualizing successful foul shots. They do it when they're not on the court and when they are; visualizing a successful shot is a great thing to do right before you take it. The same principle applies to all competitive athletes, entertainers, celebrity chefs, and everyone else who spends a lifetime trying to perfect a skill they perform in front of a crowd. They think about what they want to happen rather than what they don't, because they know that actions follow thoughts.

If you'd like to test this yourself, find the nearest two year old, hand them a glass of water, and say, "Don't spill that." When they spill it, don't blame them, blame yourself. They did what you told them to do. In order for our brain to understand a command like "Don't spill that," we first have to picture spilling it. The only way we can understand what we're not supposed to do is to picture doing it. The next time you tell someone not to do something, you're instructing them to visualize doing it.

The same thing happens when we tell ourselves not to do something. Like this:

Do not think of a purple rhinoceros.

Next time you have to do something challenging, you can think about what could go wrong, and imagine that, or you can think about what could go right, and imagine that. Your choice.

This question might help:

What if it does goes right?

When you imagine that, try this follow-up question:

How would it feel if it goes right?

If you're like most people, you've spent a great deal of your life wondering what could go wrong. Why not spend the rest of your life imagining what could go right?

8

What have I overlooked?

*W*hen I was a kid I loved to play basketball. I would spend hours dribbling, shooting, driving to the basket, and playing one-on-one with anyone who showed up at the playground. I could beat most of my friends, so I thought I was pretty good. Later, when I tried to play on a team, something curious happened: I was terrible.

My skills hadn't disappeared, but someone would always come out of nowhere and steal the ball. In one-on-one, I'd learned how to play against the person in front of me, but I'd never learned how to pay attention to what was happening around me.

It was a useful lesson in basketball but even more useful off the court. I realized that life is three dimensional, but I'd been playing in only two dimensions.

Think about a problem or challenge you're struggling with. So far, everything you've tried hasn't worked. Ask yourself:

What have I overlooked?

Listen to what you come up with. Allow your brain to turn over any rock it finds and examine what's underneath. Capture it all. When you're finished, what have you learned?

When you develop the habit of thinking in three dimensions instead of two, you'll have a profound impact on every area of your life.

Consider magicians. They make a living by distracting people. They give you something to pay attention to while they're doing something else. Con men do the same, but with a different motive. So do unscrupulous politicians. They tell you to pay attention to some shiny object, while they're busy doing what they don't want you to see.

We even do this to ourselves. If you find yourself in a situation where something just doesn't feel right, pause for a moment, take a deep breath to center your thinking, and ask:

What am I missing?

Your answers may surprise you. Our subconscious is often aware of what our conscious mind is not, but we may ignore it if we're distracted by what we think we know, without considering what we don't.

Here's a useful follow-up question:

What haven't I thought about?

And this:

What don't I know about this that I should know?

When you ask these questions, and pay attention to your answers, you may discover there's a lot more going on around you than you realized.

9

What can I do differently tomorrow?

*H*ave you ever noticed that ships are steered from the stern? Life works the same way. Tomorrow will take you in the direction you point yourself toward today. The end of each day is an ideal time to look back and ask yourself:

What would I have done differently today?

Whatever you come up with, ask:

What can I do differently tomorrow?

Settle on one thing to change. Perhaps it's your attitude, or the way you greet a coworker or your significant other. Maybe it's what you eat, watch, read, wear, or any of the other details that make up your day. Commit to taking that new action tomorrow. Put it on your calendar.

Tomorrow, at the end of the day, ask yourself:

What did I do differently today?

Then ask the obvious follow-up:

How did that work?

When you're done, start the process over for the next day.

Think of it as an action forecast. It's like a weather forecast, but you can do something about it. Before you go to bed, check your action forecast for what you plan to do differently tomorrow. It will set your feet on the right path before you even get out of bed in the morning.

10

What if I'm wrong?

*M*ost of us are willing to acknowledge at least a theoretical possibility we could be wrong. But that rarely stops us from insisting we're right.

We're know we're right about a lot of things. Politics and religion leap to mind, but we don't stop there. The best baseball team, the way to raise a child, the correct amount of spice to add to chili, and so on. In our heart of hearts we know we're fallible beings, but that doesn't prevent us from acting as if we're infallible. Although we know we've been wrong before, we're positive we're right this time.

Consider something you believe so deeply you're unwilling to consider any possibility you might be wrong. With this absolute certainty in mind, ask yourself:

How can I prove I'm wrong?

At first, you might not come up with anything. If you're sure you're right, how can you prove yourself wrong? But here's a sobering thought. Whatever you're most certain about, billions of other people disagree with you. They're as convinced you're wrong as you're convinced you're right.

This is a good time to ask yourself:

What do they know that I don't?

Listen to everything you come up with. Be honest with yourself. Allow yourself to imagine what other people might know that you don't.

Then ask:

How would I feel if I knew that?

When you're finished, switch gears and get ready for a much tougher challenge. Consider the thing you're absolutely certain about. With that in mind, ask yourself:

How can I prove myself right?

You already know you're right. The objective here is to prove it to someone else, with the kind of proof that would convince them.

Facts are a good place to start. Without facts, all we have are opinions. There's no proof in that.

Think of facts as independently verifiable information. That means the other party, the person who disagrees with you, is able to verify any facts you provide. If they can't verify a piece of information you provide, then it's not a fact; it's just your opinion.

Go ahead: prove yourself right. Jot down the facts you'd use to persuade someone else. Take as much time as you need. Remember, facts are independently verifiable by the person you're trying to persuade.

When you're finished, you may find yourself long on opinions and short on facts. Don't be surprised. The more certain we are about something, the less likely we are to rely on facts.

Certainty is based on faith rather than facts. Not faith in the religious sense, but in the sense we don't need facts to feel certain.

Quite the opposite. Facts have a nasty habit of challenging certainty, and certainty doesn't like that.

The Certainty of Uncertainty

Fact-based reasoning begins and ends with uncertainty. Facts can't prove certainty because the next facts that come along might disprove it.

That's the scientific method in a nutshell. At best, any scientific fact is a consensus of opinion about what has been proved to that point; it remains a fact only until a new fact comes along and a new consensus is formed. There's no certainty allowed. A scientific fact will remain a fact only until it has been disproved.

Faith-based reasoning is the opposite; it begins and ends with certainty. Faith remains faith as long as people choose to believe it, regardless of facts. Facts are unnecessary, if not downright objectionable, because they can challenge certainty, but they can never prove it.

When science builds a consensus around a fact, not only is the fact open to challenge, it's expected to be challenged. A fact is a fact only as long as it proves to be true. When it proves to be false, it's discarded like yesterday's news.

There's no similar process for faith-based reasoning. Certainty is all that matters. Facts can neither prove faith-based certainty nor disprove it. At best facts are irrelevant to that certainty. At the worst, facts make it uncertain.

This puts human beings in a bind. The more certain we are about something, the less likely we are to rely on facts. To put it bluntly, the more certain we are, the more likely we are to be wrong.

Paradoxically, the best way to defend certainty is to allow it to be challenged. Consider again something you believe so deeply you're unwilling to accept any possibility you could be wrong. With that absolute certainty in mind, ask yourself:

What if I'm wrong?

Listen to your answers, even if you might be afraid of them. Wait for them if need be. Ask and they will come.

Here's an important follow-up question:

What are the consequences if I'm wrong?

I like this question because it doesn't challenge our certainty. Instead, it invites us to think about the consequences of being wrong. That's powerful medicine because it allows us to contemplate the bigger picture beyond our opinions.

Whatever the consequences for being wrong, you're subject to those consequences even if you believe you're right. Like gravity; it works the same whether you believe in it or not.

As humbling as it may be to consider the possibility of being wrong, in practice it's a source of great personal power. The ability to change our mind in light of new information is not a weakness: it's a strength. Psychologists call it intellectual humility.

I call it common sense, and like most common sense there's nothing common about it. We cling to our opinions like life preservers in a hurricane. Our opinions reflect our point of view, and our point of view is who we are. To change an opinion that matters to us requires us to modify our point of view. Essentially, we have to change who we are.

That's scary, but we've been doing it our entire lives. That's where change happens. Growth comes at the expense of prior opinions. To change our lives, we have to change ourselves, in small ways and sometimes in large ways, each of which requires us to update our point of view. If you want to change your life at the speed of thought, you have to change your point of view.

One way to encourage this is to be open to new information—indeed, to solicit new information. Whenever you feel most certain about something, it's the perfect time to ask:

What don't I know about this?

Listen to your answers; they have a lot to tell you. Being human, there's a lot more we don't know than we do. Once we acknowledge this, we open ourselves to additional information. We're no longer afraid of it.

Here's another useful question:

What do I know about this that might be wrong?

Even if you have the soundest judgment, if you have bogus information, you have a problem. There's a big difference between being wrong and being misinformed. When you're misinformed, you can fix it with the right information. But when you're wrong, you're stuck until you change your point of view.

The most satisfying beliefs are the ones we open to challenge. If they can pass that test, then they're worth believing. The most dangerous beliefs are those we refuse to challenge. Even if we think we're right, we can't escape the consequences of being wrong. That's a high price to pay for a closed mind.

As the old saying goes, there's a big difference between being stupid and being ignorant. You can fix being ignorant.

How can I make the best of this?

$\mathcal{W}$ hen life gives you lemons, you're supposed to make lemonade. That looks great on paper, but what if the lemons are rotten?

If this happens to you, ask yourself:

How can I make the best of this?

Listen to your answers, even if you don't feel like listening. What do you have to lose except for the pain?

If something bad has happened to you, your first thoughts might not be printable. But eventually something you didn't expect will occur to you, something that moves you beyond despair and frustration into forward motion. Maybe it won't make everything right, but it will let you salvage what you can.

You might realize you've learned something worth more than the price you had to pay. You might find an unexpected opportunity lurking in the shadows. Or you might laugh out loud at the absurdity of the situation. All of these are better outcomes than feeling sorry for yourself.

Here's a variation on this question that might help. When the situation is so bad that all you have left is your sense of humor, ask:

How can I make the worst of this?

The creativity of the human mind is bottomless. No matter how bad the situation might be, you can always make it worse. If you let yourself imagine how bad things could be, they might not feel quite as bad as they are. Who knows, it might even make you laugh.

Either way, it's the perfect time to ask:

If I could make the best of this, what would I do?

Ask it out loud, listen to all your answers, and capture them.

The previous three questions shift your focus away from what has happened to you, to what you're going to do about it. That's how you survive misfortune. If you feel helpless, then you are helpless, like a cork bobbing on an endless sea. But if you focus on what you can do, regardless of what is happening around you, then you're still in the driver's seat.

Book 5: THE MAGIC OF HEALTH

1

How can I be healthier?

a s the proverb says, "A healthy person has a thousand wishes, but a sick person has only one."

Health is a gift you give yourself. Not entirely, of course. You have zero control over your heredity, and very little control over external threats from the environment. But many health outcomes are overwhelmingly the result of what we choose to do with our bodies. What we choose to put in our bodies. How much exercise we choose to do. How much sleep we choose to get. What we choose to think about moment by moment. In each of these areas, we can make choices that improve our health, or we can make choices that compromise our health, often insidiously.

Most of us have made some bad choices in the past. I know I have. The trick is to refuse to allow poor choices in the past to become excuses for making poor choices in the present.

If you wish you had eaten better when you were younger, eat better now. If you wish you had exercised more, exercise more now. If you wish you had never started drinking or smoking or using drugs, choose to free yourself from these now.

If you make decisions that help you be healthier from this moment forward, you may be surprised by how much your body can heal itself from poor decisions of the past. But if you use poor decisions of the past as an excuse for making poor decisions today, you may not get a second chance to make it right.

So here's a good *Magic Question* to start with:

What can I do to be healthier?

Listen to your ideas, no matter how silly or improbable they might seem. Capture everything you come up with. Then ask yourself this follow-up question:

What *else* can I do to be healthier?

An interesting and powerful variation is to ask a *Magic Question* like this:

What would it feel like to be healthier?

Go on, let yourself imagine this. Let yourself feel it. Even if you're not sure what it would feel like to be healthier, let your imagination run wild.

Motivation is less about *what* you want than *why* you want it. If you have no idea what it would feel like to be healthier, why on earth would you aspire to it?

If you like the feeling of being healthier, ask yourself:

What can I do to feel healthier?

As with all *Magic Questions*, ask these questions out loud, preferably standing up so you get your whole body into the question. Listen to your answers, all of them, even the silly or impossible ones. Capture all your answers on a piece of paper or in your note-taking app. When you're done, reflect on what you've come up with.

And always keep in mind the four shortcuts to better health:

- Eat healthy

- Exercise healthy
- Sleep healthy
- Think healthy

Making progress in any one of these areas will help you feel better, and may help you make progress in the others. And each one lends itself to obvious *Magic Questions*, such as:

How can I eat healthy?

How can I exercise healthy?

How can I sleep healthy?

How can I think healthy?

2

How can I increase my energy?

*L*ife requires energy. Every step we take, every task we accomplish during the day, every text we send or photo we share, even brushing our teeth before we collapse into bed, all these require energy. Without energy we can become depressed, which drains our energy even more and creates a downward spiral.

Better to ask a *Magic Question* like this:

How can I increase my energy?

Listen to your answers. Capture them, and reflect.

If you feel your energy level dropping during the day, ask the question again. Ask it as often as you need it. You'd be surprised how much it can perk you up. It's kind of like when a teacher calls on you in class when you're about to fall asleep. We all tend to wake up when we know someone is paying attention to us, even if it's ourself.

Here are some questions that can help you discover how energy works in your life:

What do I do that leaves me refreshed?

What do I do that leaves me energized?

When you have a sense of what works for you, figure out what doesn't:

What do I do that leaves me drained?
What do I do that leaves me deflated?

Once you know what energizes you and what doesn't, you can organize your world around the former and avoid the latter. You may have to change your schedule, not to mention your thinking. You may have to create new habits. But if you want more energy, it's worth it.

Here's a question that can help you figure out what to do next:

How do I learn to have more energy?

Listen to your answers. Think of energy as a new skill and set about learning it. There's an entire industry that can help, from books, to podcasts, to webinars. One way to discover these resources is to perform an internet search with this question as your query.

It's hard to separate energy from health. You can't be healthy without energy, and you can't have energy without health. Just as every topic in this chapter is about how to become healthier, each is also about how to have more energy, from how you eat, to how you exercise, to what you think. The more energy you have, the more of life you can live.

3

How can I eat healthy?

ood is a topic on which we're inundated with information, but woefully ignorant about how it affects our health, energy level, and quality of life. Fortunately, you have at your disposal the world's greatest expert on how food feels in your body. *You*.

Here's a *Magic Question* that can get you started:

What foods give me energy?

When you've captured some answers, ask this:

What foods drain my energy?

Listen to your answers. Listen to your body. Pay attention to how you react to foods.

For instance, I used to enjoy a glass of orange juice in the morning, until one day when I didn't have it I noticed how much more energized I felt later on. So I tried an experiment for a few days: One day with orange juice, and the next day without. Sure enough, whenever I drank orange juice I went into an energy tailspin about

30 minutes later. At the time, I didn't understand why, but I didn't have to. All I had to do was stop drinking orange juice, which made a big difference in both my energy level and my productivity.

Later, when I did some research and learned about the glycemic load that various foods deliver to the body, it all made sense. But I didn't have to do any of that research or consult some health guru to listen to what my body was telling me. Neither do you.

When you're ready to pay attention to what your body is telling you, ask yourself:

How can I eat in a way that makes me feel healthier?

Experiment until you have a clearer sense of which foods make you feel healthier and which don't.

This may be a little tricky at first because many of us eat for entertainment instead of for fuel. We choose what we eat based on how it makes us feel now, in the moment, rather than whether it gives us more energy and vitality over time, and makes us feel healthier. But many foods that may feel good in the moment are poison. Alcohol and sugar come to mind. They may make us feel good temporarily, but we pay a price later on. And the price accumulates with time until it can quite literally kill us.

If you haven't done so before this, now is the time to start devoting more attention to the price you pay for what you eat, rather than the temporary fix you get from a sugar rush or an alcohol buzz.

How can I fit healthier foods into my diet?

Too often we eat according to what others tell us is good for us. There's nothing wrong with listening to experts, but your body knows more about what works for you than any expert does.

Here's a tip: Try varying your diet and paying attention to your energy level in the moment, as well as afterwards. If you feel your body crash after you eat something, that stuff is not helping you.

In particular, carbohydrates and sugar can cause dramatic

swings in energy. But this varies widely from person to person. So you need to listen to *your* body and *your* experience. This is especially true when it comes to snacks. If you feel groggy after a Danish or a candy bar, try something else for your next snack.

Fruit is my preferred choice because it's chock-full of nutrients and fiber, and in my body it produces high energy with a low glycemic load. I get the boost without the crash. But that's my body. Your body may react differently, and that's the body you need to listen to. All you have to do is ask:

What snacks leave me feeling energized?

Habits

As we all learn the hard way, not everything that feels good is good for us. As we've already seen, many substances we ingest feel pleasant at first, but over time they drain our energy and damage our body. Especially in excess. When we're younger, we feel like we can get away with almost anything. But over time, the cumulative effect of ingesting even moderate amounts of poison can seriously deplete your health, and eventually kill you.

When I say poison, I'm talking about the usual suspects: Smoking, vaping, alcohol, recreational pharmaceuticals, and sugar. Yes, sugar. These things steal your health. If you're addicted to any of them and want to get your life back, seek professional help. If they're just bad habits rather than addictions, create new habits.

For instance, think of something you're ready to consume less of. Ask yourself:

How can I reduce my consumption of_ _ _ _?

Listen to your answers. Capture them.

This question may at first draw a blank. Not because there's nothing there, but because you're so hooked on this substance that you won't allow yourself to contemplate less of it. Your bad habit is fighting back. If you find yourself in this situation, ask the question differently:

If I wanted to reduce my consumption of ____, how would I go about it?

You can even take the question a step further:

If I *really* wanted to reduce my consumption of ____, how would I go about it?

Your mind responds differently to different *Magic Questions*, and to different ways of asking them. Take advantage of this.

And whatever questions you ask, listen, capture, and reflect. You may be surprised what you come up with.

You can also ask yourself this question:

What can I have instead of ____?

This is your chance to choose something better for you, like fruit, perhaps, or exercising instead of eating, and turn to that next time you crave what you're trying to cut back on. At first, it might feel like an unnatural act. That's okay. Keep doing it and it will become a new habit. The habit of health.

4

How Can I Get My A.S.S. in Gear?

*W*hen I reached a time in my life when I was forced to focus on my health, I'd been pretty lucky up to that point, but as the years and the pounds accumulated, I had some issues.

For one thing, I drank too much. I wasn't an alcoholic, at least as far as I understand what that term means, but I drank more than was good for me. Ironically, I didn't even like alcohol, but when I discovered tequila, for some reason I took a shine to it.

I also ate too much, and that really had been a lifelong addiction. Especially when it came to sugar and salt. Anything that had a lot of either one in it, or better yet both, and I was hooked. Especially if it was chocolate.

The more research I did on nutrition and diet, and my diet in particular, the more I realized that too much salt really is bad for you, and refined sugar is essentially poison. Given that margaritas had become my favorite drink, and were chock-full of alcohol, sugar, and salt, I realized that I was slowly but surely poisoning myself to death.

This seemed like a poor decision, so I decided to do something about it. I came up with a *Magic Question* that has transformed my life and my health:

How can I get my A.S.S. in gear?

This is one of the most powerful *Magic Questions* I've ever discovered because it covers so much ground in such a pithy fashion. The *A* stands for alcohol, the *S* stands for sugar, and the second *S* stands for salt. Here were all three of my weaknesses tied up with a neat little bow. And suddenly I had a way to handle them.

Before I finish this story, I want to make it clear that I'm not trying to change what you eat or drink. That's entirely your business. Nor am I qualified to do so because I have no credentials as a dietitian or nutritionist. Nor am I suggesting that your results will mirror mine. All I want to do is illustrate from personal experience the remarkable power of this intriguing *Magic Question,* and how profoundly it has helped me deal with a very specific and dangerous problem.

When I asked myself this question for the first time, I found myself thinking differently about all three of these poisons. For starters, I began to *think* about them. Prior to that moment, my approach to these three substances was largely a matter of habit. On any given day, I tended to do what I had done the day before, and the day before that, and so on into the distant past, for no better reason than because I had pretty much always done it that way.

But when I asked myself this *Magic Question,* the first thing I noticed was that I began to pay attention to what I was putting into my body. This seems like such a small thing, but it turned out to be life-changing. Nobody wants to be hung over. Nobody wants to be fat. Nobody wants to have high blood pressure. But if that's true, then why do we (okay, me) eat and drink in such a way as to create these experiences in our life?

Like most bad things we do to ourselves, mine was partly from ignorance and partly from habit. The ignorance was on two levels. First, I didn't really want to know how much of these poisons I was putting into my body so I conveniently chose not to pay attention.

Second, I didn't really understand how bad they would be for me, or at least I didn't want to admit it.

The habit part was just what you would expect. I had spent a lifetime learning how to eat and drink the wrong things. Making changes in what I consumed meant that I had to revise some deeply ingrained habits.

Oddly, I didn't abuse these poisons during the day. I had no urge to eat crap or drink alcohol during the workday because I was so focused on my work.

But at night, when I settled down to read a good book, or even better, watch TV with my wife, my habit was to drink margaritas, eat salty foods like pizza and fried chicken, and follow that with some form of chocolate, usually ice cream or cookies (or both).

As I write this, and read it almost in disbelief, it sounds so stupid, right? And yet it was true. For years.

Why am I telling you all this? Because you don't create health problems for yourself in one sitting. You don't gain 20 pounds overnight (although I think I came close a couple of times). But if you gain just one pound a month, you'll be a blimp in a few short years. Nobody wants to do that, but think how many of us actually do it.

And that's just the weight problem. All kinds of nasty stuff goes on inside your body when you consume alcohol, refined sugar, and salt. And when you consume them in excess, like I did, you're not simply diminishing the length of your life, you're diminishing the quality of your life. You don't sleep as well. You feel tired and sluggish. You don't think as clearly. You don't have as much motivation. Need I go on?

But when I finally asked myself the *Magic Question* above, I finally started paying attention to what I was consuming. From this alone, with almost no conscious effort, I began to consume less of all three poisons.

With conscious effort the results were even better. As so often happens with a *Magic Question*, many of my answers were more questions. If I was about to reach for something that I knew wasn't good for me (because I was finally paying attention), then I asked myself:

What is a healthier choice?

It's hard to come up with a simpler question than this, but boy did it work. It worked because it changed what I was thinking about.

Notice that I wasn't denying myself anything, otherwise it would have been a disaster. Whenever I try to tell myself not to do something, then like any normal two-year-old I'm not happy until I do.

But in all fairness to us two-year-olds, this is how the brain works. You can't tell it *not* to do something without commanding it to think about what you don't want it to do.

Here's a classic example of this from the psychology textbooks:

For the next 3 seconds, *don't think about a pink elephant.*

Okay, times up. What did you think about?

Chances are, you thought about a pink elephant. You couldn't help it because you were asked *not* to think about it. The brain is unable to process the command, "Don't think about a pink elephant" without first imagining what it's not supposed to think about. This is the only way it knows what *not* to do. The more we tell ourselves not to do something, the more we think about doing it. We can't help it because it's how our brain functions. Everybody's brain.

The beauty of my question about a healthier choice is that it doesn't tell me what not to do, so I don't have to think about what not to do. I simply have to answer a question. That's not just easy, but as we've already seen it's almost irresistible.

A question creates a vacuum in our mind. Nature abhors a vacuum. Whenever we're asked a question, or we ask one of ourselves, it's almost impossible for us not to think about answering it. So in that magical moment when we ask ourselves a question, we feel compelled to answer it, and we change what we're thinking about.

Bingo! That's the superpower of *Magic Questions!* They are the easiest way on the planet to change what we think about. And nothing illustrates this better than what happened to me when I began to ask the questions I'm sharing with you here.

Whenever I asked myself, "What is a healthier choice?", in that moment I changed what I was thinking about. Instead of gleefully anticipating a bowl of ice cream, or a chocolate chip cookie, I began to think about healthier choices, such as fruit. The more I thought about these healthier choices, the more I wanted them, and the less I wanted the unhealthy choices that had been my habitual way of eating. Not because I was denying myself unhealthy choices, but because I was thinking about something else.

Oddly enough, when I began to change the way I ate and drank, I didn't miss the substances as much as I missed the comfortable habit of consuming them. The way you might miss your favorite pair of slippers if you threw them away because they were falling apart, even though they still *felt* good.

Over time, the act of thinking about healthier choices became a new and comfortable habit, replacing my old habits. Believe it or not, this even applied to alcohol. I still enjoy a drink every now and then, but now I enjoy not drinking even more.

In my case, sugar and salt were harder to deal with than alcohol because my body really seemed to crave them. But when I thought about making healthier choices, and made that a habit, even these cravings faded. Again, not because of self-discipline, but because I learned to ask myself the right question, in the right way, at the right time. This allowed me to change what I was thinking about. When I changed what I was thinking about, I changed what I ate and what I drank. It was as simple as that.

During this process, whenever I still had a craving for something that was bad for me, this became one of my favorite *Magic Questions*:

What healthy food would I enjoy eating at this moment?

Even if my craving was strong, I couldn't help but think about something healthy, and not just healthy, but something I would enjoy. That did the trick for me. I wasn't denying myself a treat, I was thinking about a different treat.

Sometimes this would lead me to an odd choice. Like if I had a craving for a chocolate chip cookie, and I decided that lima beans were not only a healthier choice, but I genuinely enjoy them. Not exactly a direct substitution, to be sure, but it worked, at least for me. Instead of eating processed poison, I would heat up some frozen lima beans and eat a wholesome whole food that was unprocessed. And yes, lima beans are high in carbohydrates, which the body quickly converts to sugar, so you can overindulge them just like you can overindulge anything else. But if you do (and I did at first) you're still better off than if you overindulge on cookies, or candy, or potato chips, or any of the other delightful poisons we so love to eat.

The net result of asking myself these *Magic Questions* is that I finally got my A.S.S. in gear. I didn't deny myself anything, but I did eat less sugar, less salt, and consume less alcohol. I slept better, felt better, had more energy, and my thinking and memory improved.

I still have a margarita from time to time, and occasionally use ice cream as a dip for my favorite corn chips (sugar and salt right?) But these are now choices rather than habits, and this makes all the difference in the world.

I've also lost weight, but I won't tell you how much because I don't want you to think you'll have similar results. This is not a weight-loss commercial. I'm not making any claims of any kind about weight loss, or any of the other potential benefits from eating and drinking healthier. That's not what this chapter is about. It's about how you can ask yourself *Magic Questions* that help you think about what you want to think about when it comes time to choose what you eat and drink.

At the very least, these questions can give you an awareness of what you put into your body, and a fighting chance to think differently about it. And as you already know, when you think differently, you act differently. That's the magic of *Magic Questions*.

Over indulging in one form or another tends to be a common topic when I'm showing people how to use *Magic Questions*. If you'd like to join a community of good-hearted people who are focused on creating and sharing the most powerful *Magic Questions* in the world, and participate in our monthly *Superpower Coaching Calls™*, you might want to check out this special offer:

The Magic Questions® Goldmine

https://www.magicquestionsgoldmine.com/special-offer-for-readers-of-10ssp

5

How can I get more exercise?

J'm amazed how few of us genuinely understand the value of exercise, despite the overwhelming attention it receives from celebrities, health gurus, and the media. Whatever your starting place, you can feel better and more energized by moving your body in a healthy way, and turning this into a daily habit. Even a simple thing like taking a regular walk can boost your energy and enhance your sense of well being.

Here's a question to get started:

What exercise would I enjoy doing?

Some people don't like exercise. Maybe it's because they haven't discovered an exercise they like, or they misunderstand the nature of exercise.

You don't have to go to the gym and lift weights to feel good about getting some exercise, unless weightlifting is something you enjoy. You don't have to do aerobics. You don't have to run marathons or ride fifty miles a day on a bike. All you have to do is move. If you're sitting, stand. Move around. Especially if you have a job where you spend most of the day sitting. If you do, get up every

20 or 30 minutes and move across the room or down the hall. That's not all the exercise you need during the day, but it's way better than nothing.

My watch automatically tells me when I've been sitting too long. Normally, I would find such an interruption annoying, but it has saved me many a time when I've become glued to my chair for too long.

If you're healthy enough, take the stairs instead of the elevator. (You might want to check with your doctor before you do this!) I work from home, and my office is just above the stairs. Every half hour or so when I'm at my desk I head downstairs and right back up, for no other reason than to get my blood flowing again. After a quick round trip on the stairs I always feel more energized when I get back to my "standing desk", where I can resume my work either sitting or standing.

And you can't beat walking. You can take a walk almost anywhere you find yourself, at any time, at any pace, for a block or for miles, whatever works for you.

Some exercise gurus would have you believe that you have to reach an aerobic state to do yourself any good. That's nonsense. Going aerobic is great, and highly recommended if you're healthy enough for it. But any movement that doesn't hurt you helps you. Movement is medicine. You can benefit merely from walking from point A to point B—however far and however fast you do it—and by making it a regular part of your day. Here's a *Magic Question* that can help:

How can I move more each day?

Movement is so important, and so simple to do, that you might surprise yourself with how many different ways you can move throughout your day that had never occurred to you before.

As for regular exercise, most people face the same problem. Exercise takes time, and your schedule is probably already filled to overflowing, which is one reason most of us don't get enough exercise. To resolve this, consult the world's greatest problem solver, your brain. Ask yourself this *Magic Question*:

How can I work more exercise into my daily routine?

Listen to your answers. Write them down. Keep asking yourself this question, and tweaking your answers, until you come up with a way to fit regular, daily exercise into your busy schedule. I guarantee you'll find room if you want to. Just imagine how much more you can accomplish during even your busiest days when you're feeling healthy and energized, instead of unhealthy and tired. In fact, just for a moment, imagine feeling healthy and energized.

See how great that feels?

Some people prefer to exercise first thing in the morning, others at the end of the day, and others at lunch or during a coffee break. Whatever works for you, turn it into a habit, so it just doesn't feel right if you skip a day.

When you reach this point with any form of exercise, you'll have more energy, feel better, and enjoy better health. Oh, and you'll get more done than you ever thought possible.

One note of caution: If it's been a while since you've exercised, consult your doctor before you start something new. You're not doing anyone a favor if you drop dead on the bike path.

6

How can I sleep better?

*S*leep is one of the most important factors in our overall health, and yet strangely, one of the most easily ignored.

Some motivational types like to flex with this old saw, "I can sleep when I'm dead." But you'll be likely to die a lot sooner if you don't get enough sleep while you're alive.

Study after study shows the value of sleep for our physical, psychological, and cognitive health, and implicates lack of sleep in health problems from diabetes to cancer. Yet more than one third of adults in the United States don't get enough sleep.[1]

When it comes to other important health factors, such as eating healthy and exercising, we can redouble our efforts to get it right. But how do we redouble our efforts to sleep?

Even worse, when we're busy—and who isn't these days—we tend to treat sleep as a necessary evil, something we have to do at the end of the day when we run out of time and energy for more productive activities.

The opposite is true. Getting better sleep is the most productive thing we can do. When we maximize our sleep potential, not only do we feel better and healthier, but we increase the amount of energy and productive time we can devote to other activities.

Sleep potential deals with more than the time we spend sleeping; it's about the quality of our sleep. Each of us has an ideal way of sleeping that will maximize the health and energy benefits of sleep. Since that varies so much from one person to the next, even expert advice about sleep can provide only general guidance. It's up to us to figure out the best approach.

There are many resources to help you learn how to sleep better, but you might as well start with the most important resource of all. Ask yourself:

How can I get enough sleep?

Answering this question might be a heavy lift for some people because their first reaction is to think they don't have time to get any more sleep, which is why they aren't getting enough sleep in the first place.

That's just an excuse. We tend to find time for what we think is important. It helps to believe that sleep is important. If we're well rested, we'll be in better shape mentally and physically to do more of all the other things we think are so important that we're willing to sacrifice our sleep to do them. In other words, sacrificing sleep is counterproductive. Getting enough high-quality sleep is the key to crushing even the busiest days.

Here's a *Magic Question* that can help:

If I really wanted to get enough sleep, what would I do?

Give yourself time with this one, especially if you're feeling some internal resistance. The simple process of considering what you can do to get enough sleep will often help you start doing that.

Here's another useful question:

How can I awaken more refreshed?

Listen to your answers. Chances are you already know how to sleep better than you do.

For instance, maybe you shouldn't binge watch your favorite thriller right before bedtime, or eat chocolate cake while you do, or have that extra cup of coffee in the afternoon. (If you're drinking the coffee because you're tired, maybe that's a hint.) Perhaps you should exercise today instead of putting it off until tomorrow. Maybe you should get a new mattress or take a meditation class. Maybe the alerts on your cell phone keep waking you up at the most inopportune times. Maybe the blinds on your window don't do a good job of blocking out the streetlight next-door. Maybe your partner's snoring doesn't help.

Each of these things can be fixed, or at least improved. To a great extent, restful sleep is about doing a good job of managing your sleeping environment. With a little thought and effort, there isn't much about that environment you can't improve if you choose to do so.

Turn it into a *Magic Question*:

How can I improve my sleeping environment?

Listen to your answers. Capture them. Reflect on them. You don't have to fix everything at once; pick something and start there

You can also ask a useful follow-up question

If I wanted to sleep better, what would I do?

With each change you make, see how energized you feel when you wake up in the morning, and as you progress through the day.

Research can help, so feel free to ask yourself:

How can I learn to sleep better?

When you've listened to your answers to this question, turn it into an internet search.

You can also seek medical advice, but you might want to try some of the easier fixes first. Figure out how to have less light in the room, less noise, and a more consistent routine for when you go to bed and get up. You can make a good night's sleep a habit like any other habit. All it takes is practice.

Make sure there's no cell phone where you can hear it. For those of us addicted to our phones, that's hard, but interruptions destroy restful sleep. If you think sleep is more important than interruptions, get rid of the interruptions.

When you improve your sleep, you'll increase your potential in every other area of your life, and feel more energy than you ever thought possible.

7

How can I handle stress better?

*S*tress can be the great sinkhole of health and happiness. When we come face-to-face with adverse or demanding circumstances, our reptilian brain tends to shift into fight-or-flight mode. If neither is an option, which is most of the time in our contemporary world, then our emotions tend to implode. Depending on the circumstances, we react in different ways. Sometimes we feel hyper. Sometimes we feel drained. Sometimes we feel both at the same time, which is truly disorienting. The greater the stress, the greater the mood swing—and the energy swing.

There are only two ways to deal with stress: Change what's causing it, or change how we feel about it.

But let's begin at the beginning with this *Magic Question*:

What makes me feel stress?

Listen to yourself and capture your answers. The more sources of stress you uncover, the better you'll be able to deal with them. In some cases, simply becoming aware of a source of stress can help you deal with it.

Here's the next *Magic Question*:

How can I relax?

Listen, capture, and reflect. This is a broad question, but don't be surprised if you come up with specific answers.

Here's a variation:

How can I reduce my stress?

Here's a "What if?" version:

If I wanted to reduce my stress, how would I go about it?

Your answers to these questions provide insight into what's causing you stress, as well as ideas about how to reduce it. The more ideas you capture, the better. Along the way, you might be surprised at how large an impact you can have by making even a small change.

Suppose, for example, that one of the stressors you identify is the person in the cubicle next to you. They're so loud that you feel drained at the end of the day. Ask yourself:

How can I sit in a different location?

There may be several options available to you. Maybe you can move to another team, or another room, or another geographic location. Maybe you can work from home. Whatever sounds right to you, imagine yourself working from that new location and ask:

How would I feel if I could make that change?

If you experience an overwhelming sense of relief, then it's probably worth doing something about it. If it doesn't make much difference, maybe something else is behind your stress.

If you can't change what's causing you stress, or choose not to, then change how you feel about it. Think of something that's causing you stress and ask:

What if this didn't stress me out?

Or this:

How would I feel if this didn't stress me out?

The dirty little secret about stress is that it doesn't come from without; it comes from within. When you feel stressed about something, these feelings are coming from you, not from the situation. The loud person in the next cubicle isn't causing you stress—your reaction is.

Stress comes from how we interpret circumstances. Think of the difference between riding a roller coaster and falling off a building. The core experiences may be similar, but we define them quite differently.

If that's hard to accept, consider this. We all know people who seem to feel no stress at all in situations that would cause us considerable anxiety. How does a musician perform in front of a huge audience without missing a note? How does a basketball player sink a foul shot with the championship on the line? How does a kindergarten teacher handle a room full of five-year-olds? How does a waiter handle ten tables at once without going stark raving mad?

It's not that they don't feel stress; they've just mastered how to deal with stress in these situations. They've prepared their minds and bodies to handle what would create stress for the rest of us. Yet if you placed them in unfamiliar circumstances they would feel as much stress as the next person. Could the basketball player wait tables in a busy restaurant? Could the kindergarten teacher perform before a packed concert hall? Could the musician handle those five-year-olds?

Whatever circumstances induce stress in you, you can choose to think differently about them by asking different questions.

What stresses me about this and how can I change it?

How would I feel if I weren't stressed?

What would it feel like to have no stress?

How would someone else feel who doesn't get stressed in this situation?

In many cases, stress is only fear talking. Maybe you feel stress in performance reviews because you're afraid of criticism. Maybe you're afraid to meet new people, so you feel stress when you do. Maybe you're afraid to leave your comfort zone so you feel stress whenever you venture beyond it.

Here are some *Magic Questions* that can help you deal with underlying fears:

What am I afraid of?

The first step in managing fear is to identify it. Fears aren't quite as scary in broad daylight.

Then you can ask:

What if I weren't afraid of that?

Or this:

How would it feel if I weren't afraid?

Here's one of my favorites:

What if I allowed myself to enjoy the situation?

Stress isn't inherently unpleasant unless we define it that way. Think of all the stressful situations we choose to put ourselves in because we enjoy them. We already mentioned roller coasters. What about competitive activities such as athletics, or chess, or other games? What about extreme sports? What about spectator sports, where hoping and praying for our team to win an important competition can be incredibly stressful. What about playing a video game? The truth is, we crave stress. We seek it out. We pay big money and spend a considerable amount of time pursuing stressful situations precisely because we enjoy them. When you encounter a stressful situation you don't enjoy, ask yourself:

What about this can I enjoy?

The Magic Of Preparation

Some circumstances are always stressful. When you encounter these, or you're about to, you can reduce your stress if you prepare for it. Here are some questions that can help:

How would I feel if I were prepared for this?

What kind of preparation might free me from stress?

How can I be better prepared for this?

How can I prepare my body and mind for what I'm about to do?

The better prepared we are to deal with what the world throws at us, the less we'll suffer from stress, and the more likely we'll be to enjoy it.

8

How would I feel if I had all the time in the world?

While we're talking about stress, have you ever felt like you have to get something done but you don't have enough time to do it?

This is one of the most common sources of stress, and ironically, entirely within our control. Whether it's from a deadline that is imposed upon us, or one we set for ourselves, the stress comes not from the deadline, but from how we think about it.

When we keep reminding ourselves that we have to get something done before a certain time, we tend to make it less likely that we'll do so. Don't get me wrong, deadlines are very useful. They keep us focused and on track. But when they do more harm than good they're counterproductive.

In my case, when I'm feeling a time crunch I get irritable, distracted, and as the sand accelerates through the hourglass, I can become a complete jerk to the people around me. (Sorry Margie!)

I also begin to make mistakes with even the simplest tasks because I'm rushing them. So I'm wasting precious time in a futile attempt to be on time. Doesn't make much sense does it?

Deadlines are good for us, but stress is not. Deadlines keep us on track and on time. Stress does just the opposite.

So the fine line we have to walk is working to complete a task by the deadline without stressing ourselves out.

Good luck with that, right?

Not so fast. When I begin to feel rushed or overwhelmed or anxious I ask myself this *Magic Question* ™:

What if I had all the time I need to this done?

Sometimes this is all I need to get my stressed-out mind back on track. But if this doesn't do the trick, then I bring out the big gun and ask myself:

How would I *feel* if I had all the time I need to this done?

If you ever find yourself feeling stressed about getting something done on time, ask yourself this question. Ask it out loud so your brain actually hears as a question. Stand up if possible, so you get your whole body into it. Allow yourself to really *feel* what it feels like to have all the time you need.

Here's a variation that can be even more powerful:

How would I feel if I had all the time in the world?

You do, you know. You do have all the time in the world. Not because you're going to live forever, but because all the time you have, all the time any of us have, is this moment. Right now.

I'm not suggesting this as some form of mystical truth, I'm stating it as a scientific fact. The only moment that any of us can actually experience is this moment. The one you're in right now. We can daydream about the past and the future, but we can't live there.

Your heart can't beat in the past or the future, but only in the present. The only moment you will ever actually be alive is this one. So why screw it up by stressing about other moments?

When we stress about a deadline, we're dwelling on the future at the cost of the present. Ironically, the present is the only time you'll ever have to work on what you want to accomplish by your deadline.

You really do have all the time in the world—this moment—so why not allow yourself to *feel* that way?

Go ahead, ask yourself this question again:

How would I *feel* if I had all the time in the world?

Ask it out loud. Ask it standing up. Allow yourself to experience what it feels like to have all the time in the world.

Because you do, when you know how to ask for it.

9

What is my excuse?

*W*hen we do something that we know isn't good for us, such as eating too much or drinking too much or skipping exercise or whatever it might be, the excuses seem to roll off our tongue, as if making excuses is an expression of some primitive part of our brain.

Well, maybe it is, so why not put it to good use?

Next time you're tempted to do something that you know isn't good for you, ask yourself:

What is my excuse for *not* doing this?

At the very least you'll call attention, in your own mind, to what you're about to do that you'd really rather not do. Paying attention to poor choices is half the battle of making better choices.

Here's an even more effective way of making excuses work for you instead of against you. Think of something that you know is good for you, but for one reason or another it's a struggle to do it.

For example, suppose you're not in the mood to exercise today, but you know you need to. It's so easy to come up with excuses for not exercising. It's raining, it's too hot, I broke my nail, there's going to be a full moon tonight. So why not use your innate talent for making excuses—a talent we all share—to make excuses for doing what you want to do, instead of avoiding it? With this in mind, you could ask yourself:

What is my excuse *for* exercising today?

Listen to what you come up with, it might surprise you. You can even ask a follow-up question like this:

What other excuses do I have *for* exercising today?

Here's another example. We'll run out of breath before we run out of excuses for eating what we know we shouldn't eat. It's my birthday. It's a holiday. It's hump day. I've been so good I deserve a treat. These excuses tend to keep coming until ultimately we lose the battle. So why not use *Magic Questions* to help you change what you're thinking about, and focus on excuses that serve you instead of betray you? Ask yourself:

What is my excuse for eating healthy today?

And you can always ask a follow-up:

What other excuses do I have for eating healthy today?

We focus so much attention on willpower that it's easy to miss the point. What we really need is "why-power". When we struggle to do something, it's because we don't have a good enough reason to do it. Making excuses *for* doing it can help us find these reasons, and focus on the "why-power" we need to follow through.

Here's another common example. Anyone who has tried to stay on the wagon when it comes to alcohol or some other substance they're over consuming knows how remarkably creative the human brain can be when it comes to making excuses for falling off the wagon. You can turn that on its head by using the same creative part of your brain to make excuses for staying on the wagon. For instance, you can ask yourself:

What is my excuse for being sober today?

If you're truly addicted to a substance this question alone isn't likely to cure you, and you should seek professional help. But for those of us who simply overeat or over drink, you'd be amazed how powerful it can be to make excuses for doing what you want to do instead of what you don't.

10

What attitude will serve me better?

*a*ttitude is a habit. If your habitual attitude isn't allowing you to feel as healthy, energized, and vital as you would like, then create a new habit.

First, figure out what attitude will better serve you. Here's a *Magic Question* that can start the ball rolling:

What attitude would serve me better?

Listen to your answers. You don't need to preach to yourself, or try to motivate yourself with a pep talk. Just listen. Trust your gut.

Here's an intriguing variation on this question:

How can I think in a way that will improve my attitude?

Remember, to change anything in your life you first have to change your thoughts. That's what *Magic Questions* do best. If your attitude is stressing you out and draining you of energy and vitality, come up with an attitude that doesn't. Keep practicing it until it becomes a habit.

Here's another approach:

What attitude would I like to have right now?

In Chapter 3 of Book 3 *(How would I like to feel right now?)* we saw that we have a remarkable ability to choose how we feel by choosing what we think about. Attitude works the same way.

With that in mind, try this *Magic Question*:

What attitude would make me feel the way I want to feel?

When you've answered that question, try this one:

What would this attitude feel like?

Go there. Let yourself feel this new attitude. You can always go back to your old attitude if you want, so there's no risk in trying a new one on for size.

Or try this variation. In any question about attitude, substitute the phrase "frame of mind" for the word "attitude." Like this:

What frame of mind would I like to have right now?

You might come up with some new and interesting answers.

If you're not sure what attitude you have, and what attitude might serve you better, pay attention to the attitudes of those around you. Pay special attention to those who project the kind of energy and confidence you would like to have. Above all, make time to hang around successful people, however you define success. Maybe they're great business leaders, or great teachers, or community leaders, or wonderful parents. Whatever you aspire to be, spend time with people who are already there.

Attitude is infectious. When we spend the bulk of our time around negative people, who always see the glass as empty, and always find something to complain about, it's almost impossible not to let their attitude rub off on ours. But the same is true when we hang around people who are positive, who see problems as opportunities, who don't waste time and energy whining about what is wrong with their lives because they're too busy making it right.

There are plenty of both types of people in the world. If you find yourself surrounded by the negative types, whether by prior choice or the luck of the draw, you can change this. It might take some effort, but few efforts will pay greater dividends.

For example, if for whatever reason your friends and family tend to have negative attitudes, make time to be with more positive and successful people. You don't have to abandon your friends and family, you just have to abandon their attitude.

You can start with this *Magic Question*:

Who has the kind of attitude I would like to have?

When you answer this question, don't limit yourself to your immediate circle of friends, family, and colleagues. The world is your oyster. Consider anyone and everyone who exhibits the kind of attitude you're looking for, whether it's someone you can spend time with in person, someone you can read about, or someone you can spend time with virtually, via online media, online training, membership groups, even movies and TV shows.

When you find someone who has an attitude that you wish you had, remember that their attitude is only a habit, and you can form your new habit the same way they did. With practice.

When you find the attitude you're looking for in someone else, with that attitude in mind here's a great way to start each day. Ask yourself this *Magic Question*:

What would it feel like to live today with that attitude?

Practice this for at least thirty days, until your new attitude becomes a habit. And then enjoy the results that come from one of the most profoundly powerful improvements anyone can make in their life.

Book 6: THE MAGIC OF WEALTH

1

How can I make myself more valuable?

---

*W*ealth comes in many forms. For those who are unhealthy, good health is wealth. For those who are busy to the point of collapse, time is wealth. For those who are lonely, a loving relationship is wealth.

And then there's material wealth. Whatever our personal net worth might be, we tend to want more. There's lots of advice about how to become wealthy, but the best I've ever heard comes from super investor Warren Buffett, who said, "Ultimately, there's one investment that supersedes all others: Invest in yourself"[1].

When you invest in yourself, you make yourself more valuable.

As human beings we are all inherently valuable by virtue of being human. But as participants in a market economy, we are only as valuable as the market thinks we are. If this sounds cold and heartless, it is. Welcome to capitalism. But there's an amazing upside. The marketplace will pay you any price you ask, as long as you provide it with enough perceived value. As ruthless and cold-blooded as the marketplace is, if you want greater rewards from it all you have to do is provide what the marketplace perceives to be greater value.

If you want to earn more, the ball's in your court.

There are four ways you can become more valuable in the marketplace:

1. Acquire new skills (or improved skills)
2. Provide a new service (or improved service)
3. Provide new products (or improved products)
4. Do a better job of communicating your value

You can turn each of these into a *Magic Question* (e.g., How can I acquire new skills?) But before you worry about the first three items in the list, consider the fourth. It won't matter how much you increase your value unless the marketplace perceives your value. If you want greater rewards, whether in the form of income, prestige, ego gratification, or whatever else you're looking for, you need to communicate greater value from the point of view of the flesh and blood human beings you seek to serve in your market.

When I refer to the people I serve in my market I use the term "clients". For your market, feel free to use any term you're comfortable with, whether its customers, clients, your employer, your colleagues, your boss, or any other people you seek to serve. If you want to increase your value to them, and your rewards from them, first you need to understand who they are and what they want.

It doesn't take a rocket scientist to turn this into a couple of *Magic Questions*:

What clients do I seek to serve?

What value do I offer them?

Take a crack at each of these using **The 10-Second Superpower Secrets™** you learned in Book 1, Chapter 2. Better yet, use the Magic Answers™ PDF you can download for free here:

Magic Answers™

https://www.magicquestions.com/magic-answers-download

When you're finished with these two questions, ask this:

What do my clients want from me?

Whatever your answers might be, there's probably a difference between what you think your clients want from you, and what they actually what from you. Here's a *Magic Question* that can help clarify this:

How can I better understand what my clients want from me?

If this sounds like market research, that's exactly what it is. But not the kind of academic, abstract research that gives you little more than demographics such as age, education, gender, etc. Demographics are useful, but you want to dig deeper if you want to understand your clients. You want to understand what motivates them. You want to understand what they're afraid of. You want to understand what keeps them up at night. You want to understand what challenges and problems they're facing, and what opportunities they're interested in. You want to understand their wants and needs, their objectives and goals. To the best of your ability, you want to understand what they're thinking. To reach them where they're at, you want to understand the conversation they're having in their own head so you can participate in that conversation.

Fortunately, you can turn all of these requirements into the following nine *Magic Questions:*

1. How can I learn what motivates my clients?

2. How can I learn what my clients are afraid of?

3. How can I learn what keeps my clients up at night?

4. How can I learn what opportunities my clients are interested in?

5. How can I learn what my clients need?

6. How can I learn what my clients want?

7. How can I learn what my clients' objectives are?

8. How can I learn what my clients' goals are?

9. How can I learn what conversation my client is having in their own head?

The other questions are self-explanatory, but this last one is special. Whoever you're dealing with, under whatever circumstances, each of you is having a conversation in your own head. You know what yours is. But the way to any client's heart is to know what theirs is. The idea is to join them in their conversation, so that the value you offer them meet their needs. Do that and they will pay you whatever you ask.

Here's a *Magic Question* that sums it all up:

How can I live inside my client's head?

Notice I used the singular rather than the plural here. When you're thinking about your clients it won't do much good to think about them in aggregate. Think of an individual. Live inside that person's head. Figure out what you have to offer that person that they will value. The aggregate will take care of itself.

Obviously, there's a lot of work involved in understanding your clients (or customers or colleagues or patients or investors or whatever you want to call them), but your investment will pay off in spades. For one thing, most of your competition won't be doing this. Whoever your competitors are, whether they're after your job or your customers or your patients or your contributors or your investors, they will be spending their time in their own head, which is the natural state for most of us.

If you can figure out what's going on in your client's head, and present your value from their perspective, that's the single most important thing you can do to make yourself more valuable than your competition, because people pay attention to those who pay attention to them. To be seen by your clients as someone who understands them is as powerful a competitive advantage as you can create.

When you invest the time and effort to understand your clients you'll know how to communicate your value to them. Whether you're asking for a sale, or a raise, or a job, or anything else from anyone else, imagine the leverage it will give you if make the effort to understand where they're coming from and what they want.

How great would it be to communicate to your clients what you have to offer from their point of view, knowing what they need, what their goals are, what their fears and opportunities are. You'll be able to enter the conversation in their head at precisely the moment, and with precisely the message they will be eager to receive. Armed with this information, you'll be better able to answer all sorts of additional *Magic Questions*, such as:

How can I better serve this client?

How can I offer this client more?

How can I make myself more valuable in the eyes of my clients?

This last one is as powerful a *Magic Question* as there is, but you can't even begin to answer it in a meaningful way unless you understand where your clients are coming from, *from their point of view.*

With just that understanding in mind, here are some other *Magic Questions* to make yourself more valuable to those you serve:

What new skills can I acquire?

For each skill you'd like to acquire, ask yourself:

How can I acquire this skill?

Or you can focus on the service you offer your clients:

What new service can I provide?

Or this variation:

How can I improve the service I provide?

For each of these questions, ask it out loud (standing up!), listen to all of your answers, and capture them.

When you understand where your clients are coming from, from their point of view, you're in a perfect position to ask:

How can I improve me to better serve them?

This question can transform your business, your career, and your relationships. So listen to your answers and capture them. Ask this question as often as you need to give yourself a competitive advantage, and keep it.

Self-improvement is a noble pursuit. But self-improvement with an eye toward becoming more valuable to the people you serve, now that's a game changer.

2

What are my strengths?

*S*uppose you wanted to improve your social media presence with a new portrait of yourself, would you start with a good photo or try to fix a bad one?

We face a similar decision when we decide to improve ourselves. Like photos, we get a better end result if we start with the good rather than the bad.

To frame this differently, think of most of the books you've read about being a more effective manager, or trainings you've attended. Historically, the conventional wisdom has been focused on how to fix the problems you encounter in the workplace. If you take enough surveys, and identify enough mistakes, all you have to do is fix whatever is broken to move ahead.

That's so ass-backwards it's hard to know where to begin. If all you do is fix problems, you miss the opportunities for growth. If all you do is focus on doing less of what's wrong, you miss the far greater upside of doing more of what's right.

For example, suppose you manage a sales force. Pareto's principle suggests that 20% of your salespeople will produce 80% of your sales. Strangely, this is true for almost all sales teams. So what most sales managers do to boost their sales is to focus on the 80% of their sales team who are producing only 20% of the sales, because conventional wisdom suggests that the best way to increase revenue is to "fix" what the under-producing salespeople are doing wrong. Even worse, many conventional sales managers nitpick whatever their top performers might be doing outside the box, to try and force them to get with the company's official program.

But if you really want to ignite your sales, study what your most effective salespeople are doing differently from the rest. Maybe it's how they think about their customers. Maybe it's the questions they ask. Maybe it's how they communicate with their customers. Maybe it's how they bring to bear the resources of your organization to serve their customers. Most likely, it's all of the above. But whatever they're doing, it's different than what your weakest salespeople are doing. In these differences lie your greatest opportunities for growth.

Your best salespeople are the strength of your sales team. The way to dramatically improve the results of your team is to focus on what your strongest salespeople are doing right, and figure out how to do more of that, instead of worrying about what some of your salespeople are doing wrong. When you focus on your strengths, your weaknesses become far less important. Perhaps they don't disappear, but they just don't matter anymore.

The same thing applies to you if you're an individual contributor. Suppose you're a successful salesperson, for example. You're great at figuring out who your best customers are, what they want, and helping them get it, but maybe you're not so good at paperwork. As much as your customers love you, your accounting department does not. If you want to improve your performance at your job, it's a much better investment of your time and energy to get better at what you're already good at. No matter how much you improve your paperwork, that will never make you a better salesperson. But if you become a better salesperson, the rest tends to take care of itself.

Whatever you do to earn a living, ask yourself:

What are my strengths?

Spend some time on this. Listen to yourself. If it helps, ask the question this way:

What am I good at?

This isn't for public consumption, so don't worry about bragging. The idea is to identify your strengths so you can improve them. After you've captured some answers, give yourself a moment or two to reflect.

We tend to be good at what we enjoy doing, and vice versa. That makes this a useful follow-up question:

What do I enjoy doing at work?

Whatever it is, chances are you're good at it. Getting better will help you improve at your job, and help you enjoy it more. You'll spend more time doing what you like, and you'll get better at other tasks too. Competence is contagious. It's hard to improve in one area without having some of that competence seep into others.

Consider your list of strengths. Rank them. If you need a refresher on how to do that, go back to BOOK 2: THE MAGIC OF CHANGE, Chapter 2: *"How do I decide?"*

When you've identified your #1 strength, ask yourself:

How can I get better at that?

Allow your imagination to come up with as many ideas as you can during the next two minutes. Write them down and reflect on what you've got. Some of your ideas might be obvious; others might surprise you.

Whatever you come up with, you're going to go further in your business and your career, and enjoy it more, if you focus on improving what you already do well.

3

What's in it for them?

*W*hatever you do for a living, chances are you interact with a wide range of people. They may be your customers, colleagues, employees, partners, suppliers, employers, or all of the above.

When we want something from other people, we're often inclined to ask ourselves: "What's in it for me?" If you want to put your career on the fast track, ask yourself a different question:

What's in it for them?

Think of something you want from someone and ask yourself that question.

When you've finished, ask this follow-up:

What do they really want from me?

We tend to think we know the answer to this question, even when we don't, so it never hurts to confirm it. Here's one way:

If I were in their shoes, what would I want from me?

Imagine that. Then take it to the next step and ask them so you can hear it from the horse's mouth. The objective is to find out how you can make it worth their while to give you what you want. That process begins and ends with them, not with you.

Once you have a clear sense of what they want from you, ask yourself:

How can I help them get what they want?

Any business transaction is an exchange of value. Whatever you offer the other person has to be so valuable to them they're willing to give you what you want. They get to define that value for themselves.

Transactions don't have to involve money. They can involve anything of value, from time, to personal services, to advice, to anything else on which the parties can agree.

Consider something you want from a person at work. Ask yourself:

What might they want in return?

Then ask:

How can I give them more than what they want?

Too often businesses try to offer as little value as possible, while disguising it as more valuable than it is. That's backward. Instead of trying to fool people into thinking you're giving them more than what they're paying for, why not actually give them more? If you've ever left a transaction thinking you made out like a bandit, that's probably because you got more than you hoped for. It's a wonderful feeling.

Why not offer the same feeling to the people you do business with? Turn it into a question:

How can I leave them feeling they made out like a bandit?

When we exchange gifts on holidays and special occasions, we often remind ourselves it's more blessed to give than to receive. This translates perfectly to the modern economy. The marketplace rewards value. Whatever your position in that marketplace, as employer or employee, vendor or customer, consultant or client, you'll be rewarded in proportion to the value you provide. Whatever you want from others, you'll get more of it if you focus on giving them more than you receive.

Here's a question that can help you accomplish this in any transaction:

How can I exceed their expectations?

Here's an interesting twist:

How would I feel if they exceeded my expectations?

Think about it, because that's how they'll feel when you exceed theirs.

4

What is the most important thing for me to do right now?

---

*H*ave you ever finished a busy day and wondered if you actually accomplished anything? Given how crowded our lives have become, this is easy to do.

But busyness isn't the problem. The real challenge is how to separate what's urgent from what's important. Most of us do it on the fly, as a matter of habit. The unfortunate result is that we tend to prioritize the urgent at the expense of what really matters to us.

Case in point: Your boss assigns you a high-priority project that's due in two weeks. If you're successful with it you'll get a promotion. Later that day, your boss asks you to do something that has to be completed by tomorrow. Which do you work on first?

Most of us would drop what we're doing and focus on the task that has to be completed by tomorrow. That's why most of us live empty, meaningless lives full of quiet desperation.

Just kidding. But if my tease cuts close to the bone, then this might be the most important chapter in the book. "Urgent" always wins unless we make time for what's important.

When in doubt, ask yourself:

What is the most important thing for me to do?

Listen to your answers. Capture them. Rank them in order of their importance to you. If you want a refresher on how to do that, review Book 2, Chapter 2: *"How do I decide?"*

When we think about what's important to us, it's easy to get flooded with ideas. If they're all important, it's tempting to treat them all the same. But they aren't. Spend the time necessary to prioritize your list. Once you've identified item #1, start working on it. Think of it as your *First Thing*; it's the most important thing for you to do. If you'd like your life to turn out the way you want, do first things first.

Sometimes this is easier said than done. Wherever this chapter finds you in life, you probably have things you're already committed to. If your calendar is full, ask:

How can I do my First Thing first?

This is where the rubber meets the road. Your job is to make time in your life for what's most important to you. If you don't, who will?

I schedule my First Thing for first thing in the morning. That's when I'm freshest and least likely to have a scheduling conflict.

This was a big change for me. I used to read the paper while I ate breakfast. I loved it, but it consumed a large chunk of the most productive time of my day. So I changed my schedule. Now when I get up in the morning I get right to work. This small change had a profound impact. I can't wait to start work in the morning because I get to do my First Thing first. I begin my day doing what's most important to me. This is the best motivational trick I know.

Whatever time works best for you, put your First Thing on your calendar. Whether you use a calendar app, a day timer, a desktop calendar, or a clay tablet, block out time each day to work on your First Thing. If it's not something you can finish in one sitting, break it into smaller chunks and schedule these.

Schedule at least twenty minutes a day for your First Thing.

Regardless of what else is going on in your life, at least you'll make progress every day on what's most important to you. In the process, you'll turn "First Things First into a habit—one of the most useful habits there is.

When you schedule time for your First Thing, honor your commitment. For some reason, the appointments we make with ourselves tend to be less of a priority than the appointments we make with others. If this happens to you, think of a first-thing appointment as a meeting with the most important person in the world. Consider it a matter of self respect. If you don't show up for a meeting with yourself, why would anyone else?

When I schedule a First Thing for any time other than first thing in the morning, I set an alarm on my phone. This keeps me on track during even the busiest of days. I made it a habit. You can, too.

Your priorities may shift with time and context. Events, both good and bad, have a way of redefining what's important. To take context into account, ask yourself this question:

What is the most important thing for me to do right now?

Your answers may differ from what you came up with in response to the first question in this chapter. This is because you've added a timeframe.

Time is not fungible. Context makes all the difference. The thirty seconds before they close the door of the airplane you're racing to board is more important than the thirty seconds of the must-see video your friend just texted you.

When we change the context of time we may well change our idea of what's important in this moment. Throughout the day it's useful to check and see if you're working on your First Thing. This question can help:

What could I be doing now that's more important?

Or this interesting variation:

What's a better way to spend my time?

If you don't know your First Thing, your First Thing is to figure it out. Only you know what's important to you. Only you can decide if you'll ever get around to it.

5

Where do I see myself in five years?

To get where you want to be, it helps to know where you're going. If that seems obvious, ask yourself this question:

Where do I see myself in five years?

Do you have a clear vision in your mind, or is it murky and uncertain?

You are what you think about. If you know where you want to be in five years, then you're halfway there. If you don't, it's never too soon to start thinking.

Here's a similar question that might produce an entirely different set of answers:

What do I want to be celebrating in five years?

With either of these questions, you don't have to start with five years. You can ask yourself:

What do I want to accomplish today?

Listen to your answers and capture them. Then ask:

What do I want to accomplish this week?

Again, listen and capture. Don't worry if some of the same items appear on this list; keep listening.

Then ask:

What do I want to accomplish this year?

Don't be surprised if some new items come to mind.

When you finish capturing those answers, ask this:

What do I want to accomplish in five years?

When you have some answers for this, compare them with your answers to the first four questions. Notice how they change with your timeline.

Two factors influence this. One is our sense of possibility. There's only so much we believe we can accomplish today, tomorrow, or next week. But if we give ourselves five years, it feels like the sky's the limit. Unencumbered by the details of daily life, we give ourselves permission to dream.

There's no law that says you have to stop at five years. Ask this question and compare your answers to the others:

Where do I see myself in ten years?

With ten years to play with, we can accomplish almost anything we can imagine. We can go to med school, run for president, or finally paint the kitchen.

The other factor that changes with the timeline is our sense of what's important. Oddly, we tend to put important objectives farther out on our timeline, allowing them to be shoved aside by the urgent. That's a mistake we'll fix in the next chapter. For now, think of a ten-year timeline as a tool to help you focus on what's most important to do now, without worrying about what's urgent.

6

How can I focus on one thing at a time?

*T*ime management isn't about time; it's about focus. We can't manage time, but we can manage what we do with it. We just have to figure out what's most important to us and focus on that. It's as simple as doing first things first, one at a time.

The Myth of Multitasking

We live in an age of distraction. Between the constant bombardment from texts, alerts, alarms, notifications, phone calls, emails, and addictive media experiences available 24 hours a day, it's a wonder we get anything done. Sometimes we don't. Yet we're so convinced we can surf all this noise without drowning in it, we've invented a myth called multitasking. We've convinced ourselves that we can do more than one thing at the same time.

We can't. Multitasking is an illusion. Sure, you can dry the dishes and talk with a friend at the same time, but only one of those is a complex task, and that's the one that gets your attention.

We can't focus successfully on two complex tasks at the same time, no matter how convinced we are that we can. The best we can do is to switch from one task to the other, over and over again, without ever giving our full attention to either. It takes a toll on our productivity in two ways: By wasting time and by sacrificing competence.

Multitasking takes longer than single tasking, and produces inferior results. Psychologists refer to this effect as the "switching cost" of constantly refocusing our cognitive resources from one task to another and back again.

For instance, we may think we can successfully talk on the phone while we reply to a text. Sadly, we can't. All we're doing is bouncing our focus from one task to the other without fully engaging in either.

The switching cost means we do a poorer job on each task than we would if we performed them one at a time. What's more, each task will take longer than it would if we completed them one at a time. We think we're saving time, but we're actually wasting it.

Another example is when we convince ourselves we can scan a social media feed while we're having dinner with our family and somehow pay attention to both. We can't, any more than they can.

Another multitasking illusion—a lethal one—is that we can text and drive at the same time. Graveyards are full of those who've tried, as well as the innocents they took with them when they failed.

Even jugglers know there's no such thing as multitasking. They create the illusion they're doing so, but they know it's only an illusion. They focus on one ball at a time, skillfully shifting their attention from one to the next, knowing that if they lose focus, they all come crashing down.

If you want to get less done in more time, multitask. If you want to get more done in less time, focus.

Start with this question:

What one thing should I focus on now?

Listen to yourself and capture what you come up with.

You've encountered this question before, but it's always relevant:

What's the most important thing for me to do right now?

Whatever answer you come up with, that's your First Thing. That's what you work on first.

First Things can change with context. If your child needs a hug, isn't that the most important thing you can do in this moment? But tomorrow, if you have to work late so you can afford to feed your child, that may be the most important thing to do in that moment.

Whatever you focus on, focus on one thing at a time. Distraction is your enemy. The media and apps that constantly distract us are designed to do exactly that. The people who create those apps need your attention to pay their bills. They don't care if you pay yours. Their job is to grab your attention and keep it as long as possible. Your job is to focus on what you think needs to be done first and do it, one task at a time.

Focus is a skill. You can learn it the same way you learn any other skill. Ask yourself:

How can I learn to focus?

There are plenty of resources that can help: books, seminars, blog posts, online training, and advice from people who already know how to focus. To find these resources, do an internet search with the question above.

Be careful though. The Internet is an amazing tool, but it's also a great way to get distracted.

Here's a useful follow-up question (for you, not for the Internet):

If I could focus on only one thing at a time, what would it be?

Then ask this:

If I could focus on only one thing at a time, how would it feel?

Something wonderful happens when you focus. For one thing, when you know you're working on what's most important to you, distractions are easier to ignore because, by definition, they're less important.

Another benefit is you can feel both relaxed and excited at the same time. You feel relaxed because you're no longer paying attention to interruptions. That reduces stress and increases energy. But you can also feel excited because you're free to focus on one thing and do it well—maybe for the first time.

The Ivy Lee Question

There's a motivational story that's been making the rounds for the last century about an efficiency expert named Ivy Lee. [1] He was summoned by the CEO of one of the world's largest steel companies, who explained, "We already know what we should be doing. If you can show us a way to get more of that done, then I will pay you anything you ask within reason."

Ivy Lee didn't ask for anything. He told the CEO, "Write down the six most important things you have to do tomorrow and rank them in order of their importance. Tomorrow, start with the most important item on your list and focus on it until you're done. Then work your way through the rest of the list in the same manner. Don't worry if you don't finish. You couldn't finish it any other way, and this way you're always focused on what's most important. Have your managers do the same thing. Do that every day for three months. Then send me a check for whatever you think it's worth."

In three months, the story goes, the CEO invited Ivy Lee back to his office and handed him a check for what today would amount to half a million dollars.

You can turn this story into a powerful *Magic Question*, what I call the *Ivy Lee Question*:

What are the six most important things I have to do tomorrow?

Create your list and rank the items. If you need a refresher on how to do that, revisit revisit BOOK 2: THE MAGIC OF CHANGE, Chapter 2: *"How do I decide?"*

Tomorrow, work on the item you ranked number one until you complete it. Then work your way through the rest of the list, one item at a time. Don't try to multitask; that will only slow you down. Don't worry about finishing your list. Ivy Lee was right. You can't finish it any other way, but this way you're always working on what's most important to you and giving it your full attention.

7

How can I reboot myself?

Winston Churchill was one of the towering political figures of the twentieth century. He was also a brilliant writer who won the Nobel Prize in literature, as well as a talented painter. And just for the fun of it, he was a bricklayer who worked on projects around his estate. When he was asked why a man of his accomplishments would deign to work with brick and mortar, he said it allowed him to use a different part of his brain.

Why would anyone want to do that? Well, in the jargon of our century, Churchill had learned how to reboot himself. You can too, with a question like this:

How can I use a different part of my brain?

What's the first thing that pops into your mind? The second? Capture your ideas and give yourself a moment to reflect on what you come up with. Any surprises?

Choose an item from your list and ask this follow-up question:

How would it feel to be doing that right now?

That's a soft reboot. It nudges your thinking and feelings in a new direction.

To go all the way, you need a hard reboot. Choose something you enjoy doing that allows you to use a different part of your brain and do it, even if it has nothing to do with the rest of your life. Think of it as a vacation for your mind.

Even a short vacation can make a difference. Set aside fifteen minutes on your calendar. When the time comes, ask yourself:

How can I take a fifteen-minute vacation right now?

Have fun with this. Try new things. Discover ways to reboot yourself whenever you need to.

You might want to take Churchill's approach a step further. Instead of using a different part of your brain, consider using a different brain. Think of it as a costume party, but for your mind. Allow yourself to think like any persona who can help you reboot.

For example, you might ask:

How can I think like a painter?

Or this:

How can I think like a writer?

Or this:

How can I think like a ____?

If you take a break from your busy schedule to use a different part of your brain, the other parts will still be working, still thinking, still creating, but without the stress of being front and center. Then, when you get back to work, don't be surprised if you have a whole lot more to work with.

8

What's a better way to do this?

*P*rocesses and policies may seem to be set in stone, but the people who thrive in today's economy are the ones who refuse to accept that. They innovate. We tend to think of innovation in terms of technology, but we can innovate in everything, from what we do, to how we do it, to how we think about it.

Consider a task you need to complete for work. With that in mind, ask:

What's a better way to do this?

Listen to your answers, even the ones that seem off the wall. They might be the best. Capture everything.

When you're done, here's a useful follow-up question that takes a slightly different approach:

What's a different way to do this?

Notice there's no judgment here. You're not trying to think of a better way to do something—just a different way. This may be all it takes to shake loose new ideas, some of which may be even better than your "better" ideas.

Pick one of your two lists and prioritize the items. Consider the #1 item on that list and ask yourself:

How can I improve on it?

Listen to what you have to say. Capture your answers and give yourself a moment to reflect on them.

In this way, you can refine your answers until you come up with an idea that makes so much sense you can't wait to try it.

There's no need to reserve this kind of thinking for only your most important tasks; you can apply it anywhere. I like to tweak my daily workflow with a question like this:

What if I perform the steps in a different order?

And this:

How can I change my workflow to produce a better result?

Tinker, experiment, have fun.

I once finished a recreation room in twice the time it would have taken me if I'd used the proper type of power saw. Since then, before I begin a project I figure out the right tools to use.

This approach works for everything from carpentry to cooking to software. I wrote two books using off-the-shelf word processing software before it occurred to me to ask:

What tools are designed for people who write books?

As a result, I discovered a wonderful piece of software that helps me get more done in less time with better results.

But I'm still using only a fraction of the power of the software, which leads to another question I like to ask:

What can I learn about this tool that will help me get more out of it?

Were I to hazard a guess, I would estimate that most of us use no more than twenty percent of the features available to us on our cell phones, computers, software, TVs, microwaves, and every other piece of technology in our lives. Whatever you're doing, whatever you're doing it with, odds are you could learn something new about your tools to help you do it better. Little improvements can make a big difference, not only in the results, but in how much you enjoy what you're doing.

Another thing that can help is to change your perspective. Question the bigger picture. Maybe it's not about doing a task better; maybe it's about doing a better task. Here's a question that can help:

What's a better way to invest my time?

Instead of asking how to do a better job, you could ask:

What's a better job for me to do?

Or take it to the 30,000-foot level:

What's a better way for me to earn a living?

You can change jobs without changing employers. You can also change employers without changing jobs. You might as well consider all the possibilities.

You can innovate in any area of your life, from the tiniest details to the most important things you do. You can innovate at work, in relationships, as well as in who you are and who you want to be. It may mean breaking some rules or creating new ones. It may mean changing your perspective so you see problems and opportunities in a new light.

The only thing holding you back is your willingness to move

forward. If you keep doing the same things the same way, you'll get the same results. If you want different results, you're going to have to do something different. Why not better?

9

What opportunities am I missing?

A while back I was in the Outer Banks photographing ospreys. As I walked along the beach one morning, the sky shimmering in Carolina blue, I wanted to capture a dramatic closeup of an osprey diving into the surf after a fish. I'd already taken a few decent shots, but I'd yet to get close enough for the picture I wanted. The settings on my camera had to be tweaked just right. I glanced at them to make sure I was ready and I heard a splash so loud I jumped. A few yards from where I was standing, a magnificent osprey had slammed into the water. It was already flying away, shaking the sea from its wings, with a fine fish clutched in its talons. The moment was made for National Geographic. But sadly, not for me. I wasn't paying attention. I was on the right beach, at the right time, at the right spot, with the right equipment, but I missed the shot.

Instead of beating myself up, I asked:

What can I learn from this?

The answer surprised me. In that moment, I realized we're constantly surrounded by opportunities, but we miss many of them

—maybe most of them—because we aren't paying attention. Focus is a good thing, but it's not the only thing. Whatever you're doing, it never hurts to look up, look around, look behind you, and ask:

What opportunities am I missing?

Give yourself a minute or two to answer this question. Pay attention to what's happening around you. Start with your physical location and then expand to consider your work, and your life. Capture your ideas. Give yourself time to reflect on them.

If it helps, ask this follow up:

What other opportunities am I missing?

In BOOK 4: THE MAGIC OF ACTION, Chapter 8, *"What have I overlooked?"* we learned about living life in three dimensions. This is an extension of that. At any moment, the opportunities we're missing can dwarf those we're aware of. It helps to think outside our field of view.

Here's a question along those lines:

How can I recognize opportunity?

Opportunity reflects context. If you're trapped in a burning building, getting a promotion is not the first thing that comes to mind.

Assuming that's not the case, consider the opportunities you might be missing in each of these contexts:

What opportunities am I missing to learn a new skill?

What opportunities am I missing to meet new people?

What opportunities am I missing for advancement?

What opportunities am I missing to help someone else?

For any of these questions, here's a useful follow-up:

How can I pay better attention to these opportunities?

We're constantly surrounded by opportunities, only some of which we're aware of. When we broaden our awareness we can dramatically expand our opportunities.

We can even transform it into a useful question, and make it a habit to ask:

How can I become more aware of opportunity?

10

What have I got to win?

*H*ave you ever heard yourself say, *"What have I got to lose?"* As a motivational trick, it's one way to persuade yourself to throw caution to the wind and plunge ahead. But as a question it takes your brain in the opposite direction of where you want to go.

Better to ask:

What have I got to win?

When we're faced with a heavy lift, it helps to remind ourselves of the payoff. That's when our brain is at its creative best. Here's a question that can help:

What does winning look like?

There's no difference between winning and losing if you're not keeping score. If you don't know what winning looks like, how do you know you haven't already won?

Here's a useful follow up:

How will winning feel?

Allow yourself to wallow in the prospect of success. If winning is worth it, then remind yourself of that. By staying focused on what can go right, you motivate yourself to complete the job.

Book 7: THE MAGIC OF PEOPLE

1

How can I improve this relationship?

*H*ave you ever had a relationship where all you could think about was how the other person should change? As tempting as it is to focus on changing someone else, the only person you can change is you.

Here's a good way to begin:

How can I improve this relationship?

When you ask this out loud place the emphasis on "I". It's all about what you do, not what you want the other person to do. Listen to everything you come up with and capture it all. Then take a few moments to reflect.

When you're finished, here's a useful follow up question:

What can I do differently in this relationship?

Ask it out loud, listen to your answers, and capture them.

When you're finished, here's an even more potent follow up:

What do I wish they would do differently?

Again, ask it out loud, listen to your answers, and capture them. Reflect on them. Which are most important to you?

Chances are, anything they could do to improve the relationship from your point of view is something you could do to improve the relationship from their point of view.

For instance, if you think the other person should be a better listener, ask yourself:

How can I become a better listener?

You can't force the other person to be a better listener, but you can make yourself one. There's not much that does more to enhance a relationship, any relationship, than listening to the other person the way you would like them to listen to you.

The same holds if you think the other person should show you more respect. Ask yourself:

How can I show them more respect?

Likewise if you think the other person should be more thoughtful. You can't make them that way, but there's no end to what you can do to be more thoughtful. So ask yourself:

How can I be more thoughtful?

I'm willing to bet you know some answers to this one.

The new and improved you that emerges from asking yourself these *Magic Questions* will bring something different to the relationship. When you change yourself, you change the dynamic of the relationship. You give the other person something different to respond to, and they may begin to change toward you.

Have you ever had a conversation that feels like you're both reading from a script? In relationships, especially long-term relationships, both parties tend to respond out of habit. If that produces the desired result for everyone involved, more power to you. But if you want more from the relationship than reciting a script, you need to change your half of the script. You need to change your habitual behavior toward the other person. That gives them an opening to change their habitual behavior toward you.

Even small changes can ripple outward to set in motion big improvements. For example, if you always argue with the same person about a recurring topic, what if you didn't argue? Better yet, what if you asked them how you might think differently about it? This changes the dynamic instantly and puts both of you in problem-solving mode. You might get an earful about how you should change, but don't be surprised if they volunteer something they should change as well.

Whatever changes you decide to make in yourself to improve a relationship, practice them until they become habits. Consider the examples above. If it feels like an unnatural act to be a better listener, or to show more respect, or to be more thoughtful, you can practice these new behaviors until they feel like the most natural thing in the world.

If you're wondering whether making changes in you will have any impact on the relationship, imagine how you would feel if the other person made any or all of these changes toward you.

When you commit to changing something about yourself to improve a relationship, these questions can help:

How can I become better at that?

How will I know if I'm better at that?

What would it feel like to be better at that?

When you do something differently in the relationship, notice what feedback you get from the other person. The quality of their feedback will tell you a lot about the quality of the relationship.

Keep in mind that when you change your behavior to improve a relationship, you're not trying to become the person someone else wants you to be; you're becoming the person you want to be. The kind of person you would enjoy relating to. The kind of person you would appreciate as a human being. Focus on these things and your relationships will take care of themselves.

2

Who are the most important people in the world to me?

$a$sk yourself this question out loud and capture your answers. When you're done, look at the list you've come up with. Are there any surprises?

For most people, this doesn't seem like a hard question to answer. They reel off a list of their closest family and friends. Maybe their dog. But as with other questions, this one suggests follow-ups that might be harder to answer.

Consider one of the most important people in your life. With that person in mind, ask:

What have I done for them lately?

Don't focus on the things that come with the territory, such as the rituals of a relationship or the requirements of familial duty. These are expected of you, in the same way you expect them from others. Don't get me wrong; it's nice to pay the mortgage, cook dinner, take out the garbage, give birthday cards, and show up for special occasions. But those are givens; you don't get extra credit for them.

Think about the little things, the considerate things, the actions that show you care. With the same person in mind, ask yourself:

What have I done for them lately just because I care?

This might be a short list, so here's a question to make it longer:

What can I do for them right now, just because I care?

These are brainstorming questions, so allow yourself to be creative. Come up with actions that have no reason or occasion to justify them, like bringing them coffee, or flowers, or a book they might like, or giving them a hug—not because it's a special occasion, but because they're special to you.

After you've come up with a few top-of-mind ideas, consider the unexpected.

What wouldn't I normally do for them?

Be as creative as you want. The unexpected often has the greatest impact.

You might also ask this:

What do I wish they'd do for me?

If there's something you would appreciate from them, they might appreciate the same from you.

As with any form of giving, you benefit too. When you get in the habit of doing thoughtful things for others, you'll almost feel guilty because you enjoy it so much. What a great problem to have.

Here's another useful question. With the same person in mind from above, ask:

How can I enrich that person's life?

Enrichment doesn't have to be about money. It can be anything that improves the quality of life in some way, large or small.

Time

The ultimate gift we can give others is our time. In an increasingly busy world, we often organize our lives to be the opposite of what they should be. Whoever is most important in your life, chances are you spend less time with them than you do with people who are less important to you, like the people at work. Sure, those people matter too, and your job puts bread on the table. But for what purpose? If you're convinced that everything you do at work is for those you love, then you're hallucinating. There's nothing more important you can do for the most important people in your life than to spend time with them.

Turn it into a question and see for yourself. Think of someone who is important to you and ask:

How can I spend more time with them?

Listen to whatever pops into your mind and reflect on it.

Here's a question that comes at it from another direction:

What don't I normally do with them?

You know your routine, but what about theirs? What are some of the things they do that don't typically include you? Making dinner? Mowing the lawn? Helping with homework? Watching a ball game? Caring for elderly parents? Taking out the garbage? The most important people in your life are every bit as busy as you are. Imagine if you were busy together.

Consider an activity they do that you don't, and ask yourself:

What if I joined them?

You can help them or just hang out. Either way, you're doing what they think is important because you think they're important. What a wonderful change of pace.

After you've asked and answered these *Magic Questions* for yourself, revisit the title question for this chapter. It turns out there's a foolproof way to identify the most important people in your life. They're the ones you make time for.

3

How can I become a better listener?

**"I believe we can change the world
if we start listening to one another again."**

—Margaret Wheatley[1]

*L*istening is at the heart of how we relate to other human beings. Whatever we do in life that involves people, it begins and ends with listening. Listening is the superpower that can change the world. If you've never thought of it that way, it's not too late to start.

As you contemplate the central role of listening in human affairs, you might want to consider how to improve your knowledge of the subject.

How can I learn to be a better listener?

Listening is the most important skill I never learned in school. Your experience may be different than mine, but I never had a course in listening at any level of my formal education.

Fortunately, there are many informal resources to improve

listening skills, from books to seminars to online training. You can discover many of them by doing an Internet search with the question above.

While you're learning about listening, ask:

What can I do to be a better listener?

Start by listening to yourself. Capture your answers and reflect on them.

Here's a question that can help:

How do I feel when someone really listens to me?

If you've been lucky enough to experience what it feels like to have someone truly listen to what you have to say, then you understand how important that is to a relationship. You also understand something important you can bring to any relationship:

How can I help them feel listened to?

When I was in high school a few of us were invited to participate in a PBS TV show that was being filmed in their studio nearby. We arrived at the studio and the crew positioned us in pairs in front of the cameras. They gave each pair a topic to discuss and told us to obey this rule: Before you reply to the other person, repeat what they've said to you—*to their satisfaction.*

Under the hot lights, with the cameras rolling, my partner began to speak. At first, all I could think about was how to come up with a compelling response. Then I realized I had to repeat what she was saying, to her satisfaction, before I could reply. To make sure we played by that rule, one of the crew sat near each pair to act as a referee.

So I tried to listen, really listen, maybe for the first time in my life. My brain didn't want to do that. I was so busy trying to figure out what I wanted to say it was hard to process what my partner was saying.

As you might guess, she was struggling with the same challenge. In a few minutes we were laughing, partly from embarrassment, and partly because the process was scrambling our brains.

I finally gave up trying to figure out what I wanted to say and simply listened. When it was my turn to speak, she did the same. By the end of the exercise, we actually understood one another. Weird, huh?

If you want to bring similar magic into a conversation, then before you respond to what the other person has told you, ask yourself:

What did they just say?

See if you can repeat it in your mind. If you're worried how that might come across, pause for a moment and act like you're really thinking about what they said, because you are.

People like that.

It'll take some getting used to, but you can practice it while you're watching TV, or listening to a podcast or the radio. When someone completes a thought, see if you can repeat what they just said.

A word of caution here, don't practice this while you're driving. If you make the effort to really listen to what someone else is saying, your full attention will be on them instead of on the road.

When you practice this in real time with a real person, don't worry about losing your train of thought because you're listening to theirs. Oddly enough, when you really listen to the other person you'll follow the conversation better than you normally do, and your words will have far more impact on them than you're used to.

4

Who can I help?

$\mathcal{N}$ews headlines tend to focus on the dark side of human nature. There's no better clickbait than a good murder, war, or scandal. But human beings have a better side. The same DNA that programs us toward jealousy and violence also programs us toward love and service to our fellow human beings.

Whatever the news might say, people like to help people. It feels good. It makes the world a better place. It feeds something in our psyche that can't be fed in any other way. It may not make a good headline, but it makes a good life.

The challenge is that we live in a world full of need. To survive in it emotionally, we may create a layer of indifference to the needs of others; there are so many of them, and only one of us. But there's another way. We can embrace the belief that helping even one person helps us all.

Here's a good place to begin:

Who can I help?

Listen to what you have to say. Don't judge or dismiss any ideas. Write them all down.

When you have a list, ask the question in a different way:

Who needs me?

Listen, capture, and reflect.

When you're finished, choose someone from either list. With this person in mind, ask:

How can I help them?

Think of it as a brainstorming question. Don't be surprised if you come up with some unexpected answers. Listen to what you have to say and capture it all.

With the same person in mind, ask this:

What do they need?

This may seem like the same question, but it's profoundly different. Too often, when we see someone we could help, we think we know what they need, but that's only from our point of view. We'll be more helpful if we consider the question from their point of view. When in doubt, ask them. You might be surprised at how little they need, and how much it can help.

Once you have a sense of what they need, from their point of view, ask yourself:

How can I help this person right now?

Those last two words are important. Good intentions are nice, but action is what makes the difference.

Here's a useful variation on this question:

How can I make a positive difference in this person's life right now?

Whatever we choose to do, for whomever we choose to do it, we always get more than we give. Helping other people is the most selfish thing we can do, but it's the best kind of selfish there is.

To help others, you don't have to sell all your belongings and give the proceeds to charity. All you have to do is make it a habit to help at least one person every day. Practice until it becomes second nature.

Here's a great way to start the day:

Who can I help today?

You don't have to do something dramatic to make a difference in another person's life. You could hold the door for someone struggling with packages. You could truly listen to someone, without passing judgment or inundating them with advice. Just listen. You could keep some small bills in your wallet in case you encounter someone who needs those few dollars more than you do, or to put in the tip jar at your favorite carry out. You could allow another driver to cut in front of you, or let a fellow shopper go ahead of you at the checkout counter. You could carve out a small part of your week or month or day to volunteer. The point is, you don't have to scour the globe to find people to help. You can help the person right in front of you.

The same applies at work. Everyone can use a helping hand; why not yours? If you want to stand out in your job, help someone else do theirs. Maybe you could help with a project or serve as a mentor. Maybe you could volunteer to do something that's not part of your job description.

In many cases, what a person needs most is kindness. This requires so little of us, yet it means so much. Imagine a time when you were in a moment of crisis and a stranger showed you a random act of kindness. If that's never happened to you, imagine how you would feel if it did.

Ask yourself:

Who can I be kind to today?

And this:

What kindness can I show that person?

When I'm most stressed, one thing that never fails to make me feel better is to smile a genuine smile at someone, or say a heartfelt thank you, or pay attention to another human being as if in that moment they're the most important person on the planet. Because in that moment, they are.

In a world that often feels like it's coming apart at the seams, kindness is the magic that can hold it all together.

5

Who can help me?

$\mathcal{W}$hatever you want to accomplish in your career, whatever changes you want to make in your life, someone else can help. Maybe all you need is a sounding board. Maybe you'd like them to play a more active role by introducing you to key people, coaching you, or providing financial backing. Whatever you need, someone else can help you get it.

Think of something you want to make happen in your life. With that in mind, ask yourself this question:

Who can help me?

This is where imagination comes in. When we think of asking someone for help, we tend to think of the people around us. However, they might not be who we need. The best person to ask for help is someone who has already done what you hope to do. If you want to learn how to play a musical instrument, it won't do much good to ask for help from someone who's tone deaf. If you want to become an investment banker, you won't get far by asking a web designer. If you want a promotion, it wouldn't make sense to ask someone who was recently fired from your company.

Here's a way to identify people who can help you:

Who has done what I want to do?

You don't have to know someone to ask them for help. In my family, there's a recent college graduate who wants to be a sportswriter. He decided to ask for help from broadcasters with the professional teams in his city, even though he didn't know any of those folks personally. Immediately, one of the TV broadcasters replied and asked for a resume so he could show it around. The baseball team he broadcasts had just won the World Series.

When I heard that story, I was delighted with the result. But I was positively blown away with the initiative shown by someone fresh out of school who decided to reach out to those at the top of his chosen profession, people he didn't know, and ask for a helping hand. I wasn't at all surprised that someone offered to help him. People are like that, even successful ones.

When you've determined who can help you, figure out what to ask them for. Here's a good place to start:

What do I want that person to do?

If you don't know what you want someone to do for you, how can they do it?

Here's a variation on this theme:

What do I want from them?

When you know whom to ask for help, and what to ask for, there's one more duck to get in a row:

How can I make it worth their while?

Some people will help you out of the goodness of their heart, like that broadcaster. Others will expect you to sweeten the deal. Here's a question that can help:

What can I offer them that would inspire them to help me?

When we think of transacting business with someone else, we often default to money changing hands. That's one way to do it. But money is only one of the things that people value.

Imagine there's a successful couple you know who could offer you advice, connections, or maybe invest in a business idea you have. You probably don't have enough money to make it worth their while, so find something else they value:

What do they need that I can provide?

Suppose that same couple has three kids and constantly struggles to find responsible babysitters. For parents in that situation, a good babysitter is worth more than money. Imagine how grateful they would be if you offered to babysit.

And that's only one of the services you might provide. Maybe they need someone to watch their house when they go on vacation, or someone to bake cookies for the bake sale at their children's school. Maybe they need their house painted. Or maybe they need advice about something you're particularly well versed in. Remember, you're an expert in whatever you know well. You might have the very expertise those folks are looking for.

There are so many creative ways we can help other people get what they want from life. Not only does it feel good to do it, it inclines them to help us.

6

If I were that person, how would I feel?

$\mathcal{W}$hen we struggle in a relationship, it may be because we can't understand where the other person is coming from. It begs an interesting question:

What's their point of view?

It's a clever saying, but we can't actually walk a mile in someone else's shoes. Nevertheless, we can make the effort to understand where they're coming from.

Consider a relationship you're having trouble with. Ask yourself:

If I were that person, how would I feel?

Listen to yourself. Try to imagine what life would be like from the other person's point of view.

When we change our point of view, we change our experience of the world. Not only can it work magic in a relationship, but it's one of the greatest gifts we can give ourselves. Emperor Charlemagne is reputed to have said, "To have another language is to possess a second soul." That's how I feel about exploring another point of view.

Here's a question that can help you begin to understand how someone else sees the world:

If I were that person, how would I want to be treated?

Or this:

If I were coming from where they are, how would I want to be treated?

If this sounds suspiciously like the Golden Rule, it's the same principle, one that's found in all the world's great religions. You can even turn the Golden Rule into a *Magic Question*:

How can I do unto others as I would have them do unto me?

The challenge is to approach this from the other person's point of view, rather than your own:

If I were that person, what would I want?

If I were that person, what would I need?

If I were that person, how would I feel?

If I were that person, what would I want me to do?

Often, when we're struggling in a relationship, we don't understand why the other person is doing what they're doing. That's a good time to ask:

If I were that person, what would I do?

Or this:

If I were that person, how would I act?

Here's a different approach:

What am I missing that they aren't?

And this:

What are they experiencing that I'm not?

And this:

What are they feeling that I'm not?

You don't have to ask all of these questions in every relationship, but if you try them at one time or another, you'll have a better sense of which to use in a given situation.

Here are two questions that get to the heart of any relationship:

How does this person want to be treated?

And this:

How does this person want to be understood?

If it seems like a lot of effort to understand the other person, imagine how you would feel if the other person made a similar effort to understand you.

The Golden Rule inspires us to treat others as we would have them treat us. But that's not the whole answer. We're all different. We don't necessarily want the same things or want to be treated the same way. The real breakthrough comes from answering this question:

How does this person want to be treated from their point of view, rather than mine?

7

What is really going on?

*C*ommunication is hard because we spend our lives jumping to conclusions. If your significant other came home with lipstick on their cheek, what would you assume?

Your answer says more about you than it does about them.

Through eons human beings have evolved mental shortcuts that allow us to process more information than we could otherwise handle. These shortcuts include a tendency to *distort* our perception of reality, *delete* information that doesn't conform to our model of the world, and *generalize* our knowledge of one thing to everything else we've lumped into the same category. These shortcuts allow us to make assumptions and reach conclusions that save us considerable time and effort in processing the enormous complexity of our environment.

Unfortunately, we often jump to the wrong conclusions. We generalize, distort, and delete our way to assumptions that make sense from our point of view. In the process, we try to relate to people who generalize, distort, and delete their way to assumptions that make sense from their point of view. It's a wonder any of us ever understands anyone else.

For instance, in a convenience store suppose we see a teenager slip a candy bar into his pocket. We may distort the truth and assume he's a thief because we didn't see him pay for it while we weren't watching. We listen to a news broadcast and unconsciously delete information that might contradict what we believe. We tune in to a political convention on TV, and in a heartbeat, we generalize about thousands of people.

Consider something as simple as a ballgame. When it's over, one side has won and the other has lost. One side is elated. The other is disappointed—perhaps angry. If an official made a controversial call, one side saw it as appropriate, while the other was convinced it was criminally stupid. Both sides witnessed the same game, the same plays, and the same score, but their experience of the event is profoundly different. What really happened? It all depends on their point of view.

All relationships consist of people who delete, distort, and generalize their way to what are often the wrong conclusions, so they can relate to others who are doing the same thing. If you find yourself struggling in a relationship, it helps to keep that in mind. You might even cut the two of you some slack by asking more useful questions.

For example, imagine that one day at work your boss asks you when you'll complete the project you've been assigned. You feel badgered and come up with a snarky response. This is a good time to ask yourself:

What's going on with me?

Maybe you're having a bad day. Maybe you're dealing with personal problems. Maybe you misunderstood your boss's intent. To clarify, you might ask yourself:

What conclusion did I jump to?

Or this:

What assumption did I make?

You might try to recover deleted information:

What am I missing here?

You might try to unravel distortion:

What's a more helpful explanation?

These are questions that can help you understand what you may have deleted, distorted or generalized into a toxic assumption. For instance, you may be overly sensitive to what you think of as micromanaging because you've generalized all questions from bosses into the category of badgering. But this boss might want nothing more than to answer a question they've been asked by their boss, a question only you can answer. Or you might have forgotten—in other words, you might have deleted from your thinking—that you had an agreement with your boss to provide a status report today. Or you might have distorted your boss's request into a general displeasure with your work when, from their point of view, it was no such thing.

When you have a clearer sense of where you're coming from, and more constructive alternatives of where your boss might be coming from, you can ask yourself:

What do I really want to say here?

Or this:

What do I really want to do here?

The idea is to think these things through before you say something stupid or do something worse. But if you do it anyway, it never hurts to offer a suitable apology, and start the conversation over from a better place—a more informed place.

In any conversation or relationship, feel free to rediscover information your brain has deleted, distorted, and generalized:

What do I really want here?

What am I really after here?

What am I trying to accomplish here?

What's motivating me here?

For extra credit, ask yourself each of these questions about the other person. Your answers will be assumptions, but making the effort to understand where they're coming from can help you right the relationship before it goes wrong.

Here's one of the most useful questions for gaining insight into what's really going on in a relationship:

How would I react to me?

If you wouldn't react well to what you're saying and doing, that gives a sense of why the other person might not.

When you're struggling to relate to someone, here are some questions that can help you take a quick inventory of what's really going on:

What am I thinking that isn't useful here?

What am I feeling that isn't useful here?

What am I doing that isn't useful here?

Whatever you're thinking, feeling, or doing, if it's not helping the relationship, try another approach.

Ask yourself:

What can I do differently here?

The first step in any relationship is to understand where you're coming from. From there, you can do your best to understand where the other person is coming from. The quality of the relationship will boil down to how each of you perceives what's really going on. The bigger the gap between your perception of reality and theirs, the more likely your relationship is headed in the wrong direction. *Magic Questions* can help you turn it around.

8

How can I find common
ground?

---

*W*e're programmed by our DNA to notice exceptions. Imagine being an ancient human crossing the African savanna two million years ago. The grasslands stretch before you in every direction as far as the eye can see, but the moment something moves, your attention is drawn to it like a searchlight. Maybe it's a predator, or maybe it's prey. Either way, you have a better chance of surviving until tomorrow if you see it before it sees you.

Consider how this instinct translates into modern life. When we're kids, the first thing we're likely to notice about others is what's different about them, and that's the first thing they're likely to notice about us. No wonder conformity is such a strong impulse for children.

As adults, when we walk into a conference room surrounded by chairs we notice the one chair pulled away from the table. When we have a performance review that is 99% positive we remember the 1% that isn't. Even the cliché that "opposites attract" demonstrates how devoted we are to exceptions. What draws two people together is what they have in common, but when we see them together, we notice how they're different.

When we have a disagreement or conflict with others, our

instinct is to focus on our differences. Think how much harder that makes it for us to find common ground.

We can't reprogram our DNA, but we can reprogram our habits. The human intellect can choose to override the human genome.

We can start by asking a useful question. Consider someone with whom you have a disagreement. With that person in mind, ask yourself:

What do we have in common?

The answers might not leap out at you. When we're at odds with someone, it can be hard to admit that we have anything in common. But we do—far more than what makes us different, if we only look for it. Give yourself at least a couple of minutes to consider that.

When you're finished, ask this follow-up question:

What else do we have in common?

Make it a habit to find common ground. If you practice it with everyone you meet, you'll start to notice a difference in how you relate to other people, and they you. For one thing, you'll have more to talk about. There's no better conversation starter than to discuss what you have in common. With practice, you'll begin to realize how much you have in common with everyone you meet, including those you disagree with. You may even find it harder to disagree with them, and they with you. Not because your differences disappear, but because you're not focusing only on your differences anymore; you're also focusing on what you have in common.

When you meet someone, or you're trying to get to know someone better, make it a point to look for areas of shared experience:

What do we have in common about our backgrounds?

What do we have in common about our families?

What do we have in common about how we approach work?

What do we have in common about how we approach life?

What do we have in common about where we grew up?

What do we have in common about our education?

What do we have in common about ____? (music, food,
entertainment, hobbies, etc.)

Here are two questions that can help you navigate even the most irreconcilable of differences:

What values do we have in common?

And this:

What beliefs do we have in common?

When you start looking for what you have in common with others, you'll find new ways to move difficult conversations forward. For one thing, when you know you share some interests and background, you'll tend to take it easier on the other person. For another, you'll have a jumping-off place for whatever disagreement you're trying to resolve. If you discover something you have in common, then maybe you aren't as far apart as you thought.

When you disagree with someone, you already have something

in common: you disagree. With this in mind, consider what you disagree about and ask yourself:

What do we have in common about that?

Looking for common ground does the most good where we least expect to find it.

Consider two of the most controversial topics: Religion and politics. If we disagree with someone about religion, we may yet have some beliefs in common. Perhaps both of us believe in God, or disbelieve. Maybe both of us believe in free will. Maybe both of us believe in the right of the other to believe whatever they choose.

That's the common ground at the heart of American politics. The only way I can guarantee my freedom is to guarantee yours, and vice versa. Why not celebrate that? Why not make it the starting point for all our religious and political discussions?

Imagine if we began every such conversation with this question:

What do we agree on?

The most profound disagreements don't seem insurmountable when we establish common ground. Differences don't feel so different when we realize what we have in common.

Something amazing happens when you build a relationship on common ground: Respect. The more we realize we have in common with someone else, the more we tend to respect that person. If you had the choice of dealing with someone who showed you respect or someone who didn't, which would you choose?

Imagine a relationship built on a bedrock of respect and common ground. Then imagine all your relationships are like that. You can make it happen if you make it a habit to look for common ground.

9

Is it worth it?

When we buy something—a phone, a TV, a car—we have an idea if it's worth the price. But what about the choices we make elsewhere in life, the ones we can't evaluate in dollars and cents? Like with people.

From time to time in a relationship, we get locked into a course of action that we feel compelled to pursue, regardless of the consequences. Maybe we're angry, or trying to win an argument, or fighting a political battle at work. If you're in a situation like that, do yourself a favor and ask:

Is what I'm doing worth it?

Some battles are not worth winning. Is it worth losing a friendship to prove yourself right? Is it worth hurting a loved one because you're angry? Is it worth putting your job at risk to insist on doing things your way?

Whatever the circumstances, you can gain much-needed perspective when you pause long enough to ask:

What are the consequences of doing this?

Behavior has consequences. In the heat of the moment, we don't always think about that, but we should. We would do well to ask ourselves point-blank:

Is what I'm doing helping this relationship?

If not, ask this follow-up question:

What is a better way to proceed?

Even in the heat of battle, you can make a different choice—a more thoughtful choice. If you change your behavior, you change the consequences.

This question can help:

What can I do that will produce the results I want?

If what you're doing isn't worth it, choose what is.

10

Who inspires me?

$\mathcal{T}$he ancient greek philosophers advised us to "Know thyself."[1] One of the most useful ways to know who you are is to consider the people you admire. They give you insight into who you want to be.

Consider this question:

Who inspires me?

Listen to what you have to say. The names you come up with don't have to be famous. I'm constantly inspired by my family and friends. When you're finished, pause a moment and reflect on the names you've written down.

When we think about people who inspire us, it brings a little of their magic into our heart. For instance, when we think about Mother Theresa, we wonder how it must feel to help people the way she did. When we see a child solving a problem in an inspiring way, we wonder what life looks like from their youthful perspective. When we think about any inspiring leader, performer, writer, artist, activist, or colleague, what we admire about them is often something we'd like to add to our own lives.

Choose someone from the list you created, and ask:

What inspires me about that person?

How you answer this says more about you than about them. We admire a trait or an achievement in someone else because it strikes a chord in us. A part of who they are touches a part of who we are.

Next, ask yourself:

How can I bring what I admire about them into my life?

I've never read good writing without wondering how I could improve my own, or listened to a moving speech without wondering how I could speak better, or been inspired by a humanitarian without wondering how I could be a little more human to the people around me. When I began to understand the power of *Magic Questions*, I would think of someone I admired and ask myself:

What can I learn from them?

You can learn from anyone; why not learn from someone you admire? Ask questions that help you identify people who have something to teach you.

Who's accomplished what I would like to accomplish in life?

Who's the kind of person I would like to be?

Who's the kind of butcher, baker, or candlestick maker I'd like to be?

When you take the time to answer these questions, you'll have a pretty good idea how to inspire yourself.

EPILOGUE

"We live in worlds our questions create."

David Cooperrider[1]

I didn't want to point this out at the beginning of the book because it would have been hard for most readers to believe, but now that we've come this far together I want to share this with you as simply and plainly as I know how:

We begin to change our lives the moment we ask ourselves questions, *simply from asking ourselves questions.*

The moment of inquiry is the moment change begins. The act of asking ourselves the right question, in the right way, at the right time begins the process of change instantly, because questions change what we think about. Questions change our point of view. Questions change our thoughts, which in turn change our actions.

And our lives.

Literally and figuratively, *Magic Questions* empower us to change our lives at the speed of thought.

EPILOGUE

With this in mind, I invite you to ask yourself the final *Magic Question* in this book, as well as the most important:

What world will I create with my *Magic Questions?*

Thanks for reading this!

Thanks for reading 10-SECOND SUPERPOWER!

If you've found it useful, please post a comment on Amazon. Here's the link:

10-SECOND SUPERPOWER

https://a.co/d/8zdvxov

A review means the world to me as an author, and it's also a great way to spread the word to others who might benefit from this unique book.

Footnotes

Prologue

1. "80 Moments That Shaped the World." British Council. Archived from the original on June 30, 2016. Cited by Wikipedia, https://en.wikipedia.org/wiki/Tim_Berners-Lee#cite_note-43.

1. How can I change my life at the speed of thought?

1. King James Bible, Book of Proverbs, Chapter 23, Verse 7

2. The 10-Second Superpower Secrets

1. *Disclosing information about the self is intrinsically rewarding*, Diana I. Tamir and Jason P. Mitchell; Proceedings of the National Academy of Sciences of the United States of America, May 22, 2012.
2. Vicki G. Morwitz, Eric Johnson and David Schmittlein, *Journal of Consumer Research*, Vol. 20, No. 1 (June 1993), pp. 46-61, as referenced in *The Science of Selling*, by David Hoffeld, p. 101, TarcherPerigee, NY, 2016.
3. Greenwald, Anthony & G. Carnot, Catherine & Beach, Rebecca & Young, Barbara. (1987). "Increasing Voting Behavior by Asking People If They Expect to Vote." *Journal of Applied Psychology*. 72, 315-318, as referenced in *The Science of Selling*, by David Hoffeld, p. 101, TarcherPerigee, NY, 2016.

8. What else?

1. Walter Isaacson; *Einstein: His Life and Universe*. (New York, Simon & Schuster, 2007).

1. How do I create new choices?

1. Descartes, René, Discourse on the Method of Rightly Conducting One's Reason and of Seeking Truth in the Sciences (1637).
2. Richard Bandler and John Grinder, Reframing: Neuro-Linguistic Programming and the Transformation of Meaning (Moab: Real People Press, 1982)

Footnotes

3. What if I can't?

1. William Shakespeare, *Measure for Measure*, Act 1 Scene 4.

4. How can I change my habits?

1. Addictions are another matter, and beyond the scope of this book. You can't give up an addiction as easily as you can change a habit, but you can decide to do something about it. You can choose to recognize that you have a problem and seek help. When you kick the addiction, you can use *Magic Questions* to help you create new habits that will help keep you free and clear.

5. What is my opinion?

1. This estimate comes from a Wikipedia piece on religions of the world: https://en.wikipedia.org/wiki/List_of_religions_and_spiritual_traditions
2. You can find this famous Platonic dialogue on the web at: http://www.perseus.tufts.edu/hopper/text?doc=plat.+apol.+38a From Plato in Twelve Volumes, Vol. 1 translated by Harold North Fowler; Introduction by W.R.M. Lamb. Cambridge, MA, Harvard University Press; London, William Heinemann Ltd. 1966.

3. How can I change my habits?

1. "Careers and Learning: Real Time, All the Time 2017 Global Human Capital Trends," *Deloitte Insights*, February 28, 2017.

6. How can I sleep better?

1. https://www.cdc.gov/media/releases/2016/p0215-enough-sleep.html

1. How can I make myself more valuable?

1. Forbes Magazine, 100th Anniversary Edition, September 19, 2017

6. How can I focus on one thing at a time?

1. I've found this referenced in a number of motivational books going back a hundred years, but I first heard the story on an audio recording by Earl Nightingale, *Lead the Field;* Nightingale-Conant, Chicago, IL.

3. How can I become a better listener?

1. Dr. Margaret Wheatley, https://margaretwheatley.com/books-products/books/turning-one-another/

10. Who inspires me?

1. Wikipedia has an interesting article on the sources of this aphorism: https://en.wikipedia.org/wiki/Know_thyself#:~:text=dialogue%20with%20Euthydemus.-,By%20Plato,it%20to%20motivate%20his%20dialogues.

EPILOGUE

1. David L. Cooperrider, https://davidcooperriderai.co/appreciative-inquiry-in-a-broken-world/

About the Author

Keith Ellis is the #1 Superpower Coach™ in the world, a #1 bestselling author, and founder of **The Magic Questions® Goldmine**, a unique online community of good-hearted people who are creating and sharing the most powerful *Magic Questions* in the world.

You can join him in this game-changing online experience right here, and take advantage of a once-in-a-lifetime offer:

The Magic Questions® Goldmine

https://www.magicquestionsgoldmine.com/special-offer-for-readers-of-10ssp

Keith also reinvented the art and science of setting goals in his classic: **THE MAGIC LAMP**: *Goal Setting for People Who Hate Setting Goals*, a book that's helped tens of thousands of readers around the world in half a dozen languages.

In addition to his books to help readers take their lives to a whole new level, he has written a bestselling thriller, **NO SECRETS**, an electrifying novel that's been called "a thrill ride on steroids."

facebook.com/KeithEllisMagic

linkedin.com/in/KeithEllisMagic

Also by Keith Ellis

THE MAGIC LAMP:

Goal Setting for People Who Hate Setting Goals

https://amzn.to/3wYbau0

With tens of thousands of readers in half a dozen languages around the world, this is the classic book for people who hate to set goals. If that sounds like you, then this powerful book will change how you think about goals—and success—for good.

NO SECRETS

A John Thunder Thriller

https://amzn.to/32iaUb2

☆☆☆☆☆ "NO SECRETS is a thrill ride on steroids! What brilliant writing! My mission now is to buy all his books and read them as fast as I can.—E.M. Alan

☆☆☆☆☆"WARNING! Don't begin to read this book unless you are prepared to read it all, RIGHT NOW! I literally couldn't put it down—and I read it twice!"

—J.W. Leeger

☆☆☆☆☆"This would make a movie that would put Indiana Jones to shame."

—R. J. Bochner

☆☆☆☆☆"John Thunder is one of my favorite fictional heroes of all time!"

—G.B. Banks

Special Offer for Readers of This Book

People learn the game-changing secrets of the *10-Second Superpower*™ in different ways. Some like to read. Others prefer an audiobook. And some would rather work directly with the #1 Superpower Coach™ in the world and bestselling author Keith Ellis, within a community of good-hearted people who are creating and sharing the most powerful *Magic Questions* in the world.

If you'd like to join Keith in this groundbreaking online experience, visit here to claim this once-in-a-lifetime offer:

SPECIAL OFFER:

The Magic Questions® Goldmine

https://www.magicquestionsgoldmine.com/special-offer-for-readers-of-10ssp

If you have more time to listen than to read, you can take advantage of a limited-time-only offer for the audiobook version of

10-SECOND SUPERPOWER, narrated by the author, Keith Ellis, the #1 Superpower Coach™ in the world:

SPECIAL OFFER for the audiobook

https://www.10secondsuperpower.com/special-offer-for-audiobook

If you'd like another copy of this book, or to give one as a gift, you can find it on Amazon here:

10-SECOND SUPERPOWER

https://a.co/d/8zdvxov